I0698373

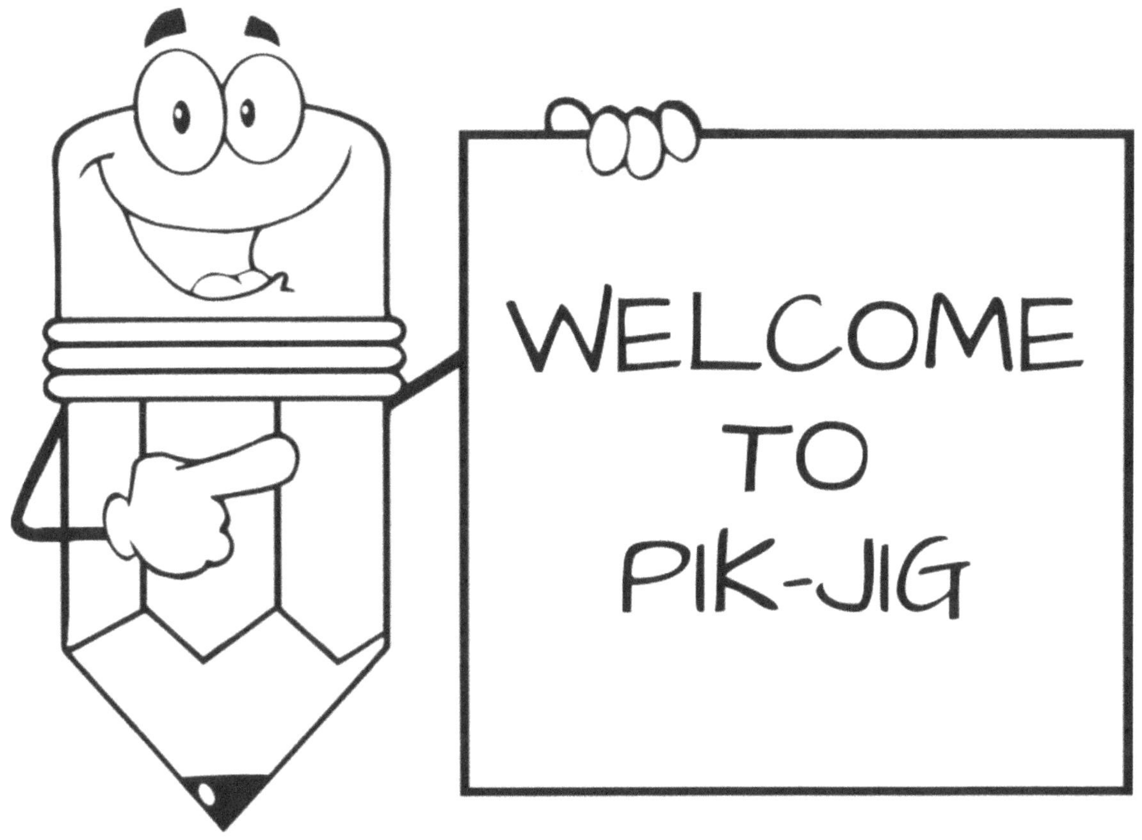

WELCOME
TO
PIK-JIG

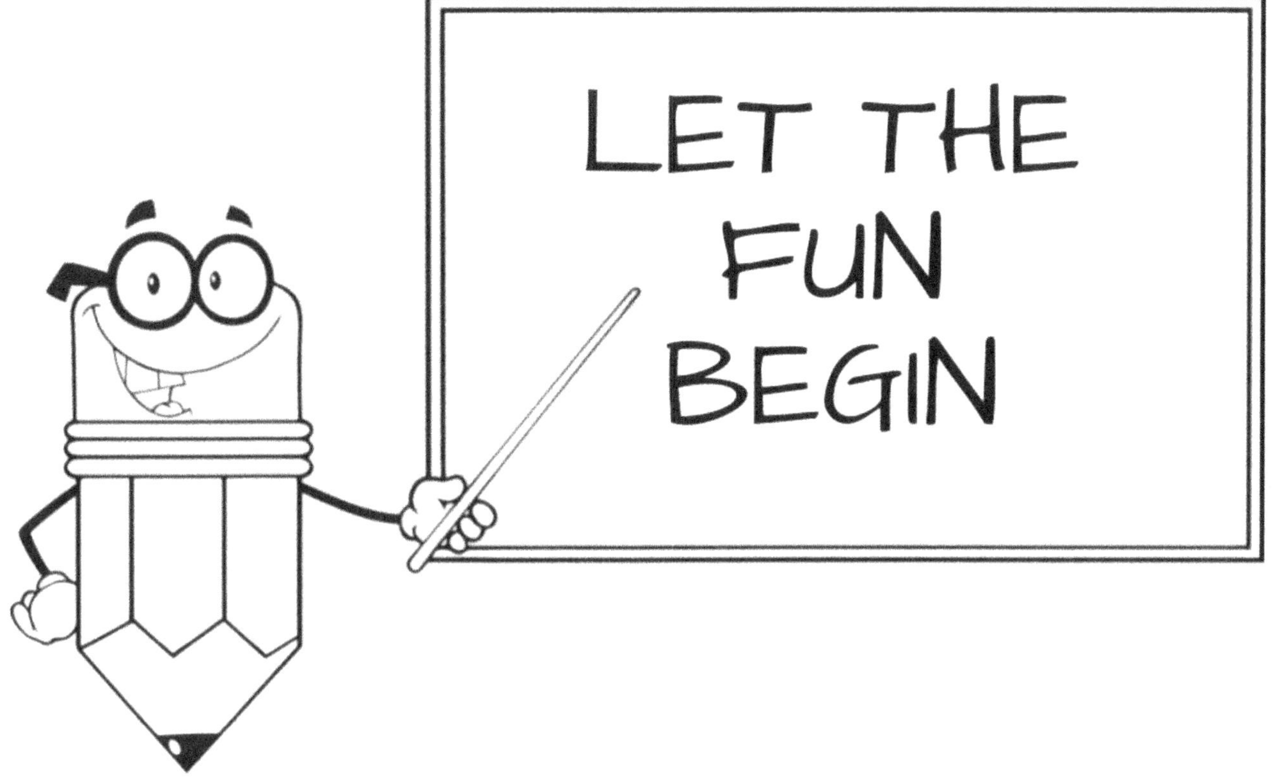
LET THE
FUN
BEGIN

INSTRUCTIONS

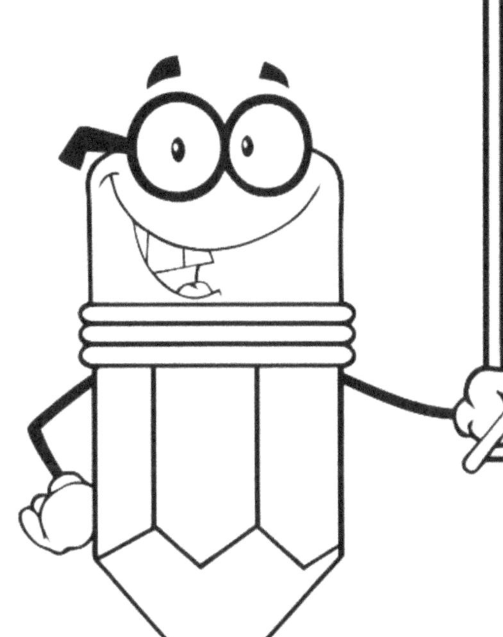

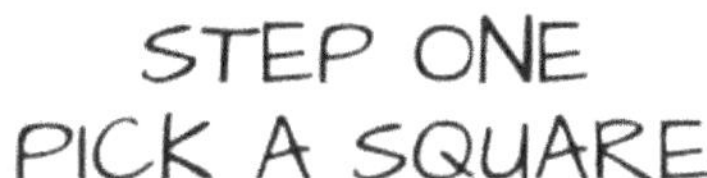

STEP ONE
PICK A SQUARE

STEP TWO
FIND THE SQUARE ON THE GRID BY
MATCHING THE COORDINATES

STEP THREE
DRAW WHAT YOU SEE AND WATCH
THE MAGIC UNFOLD

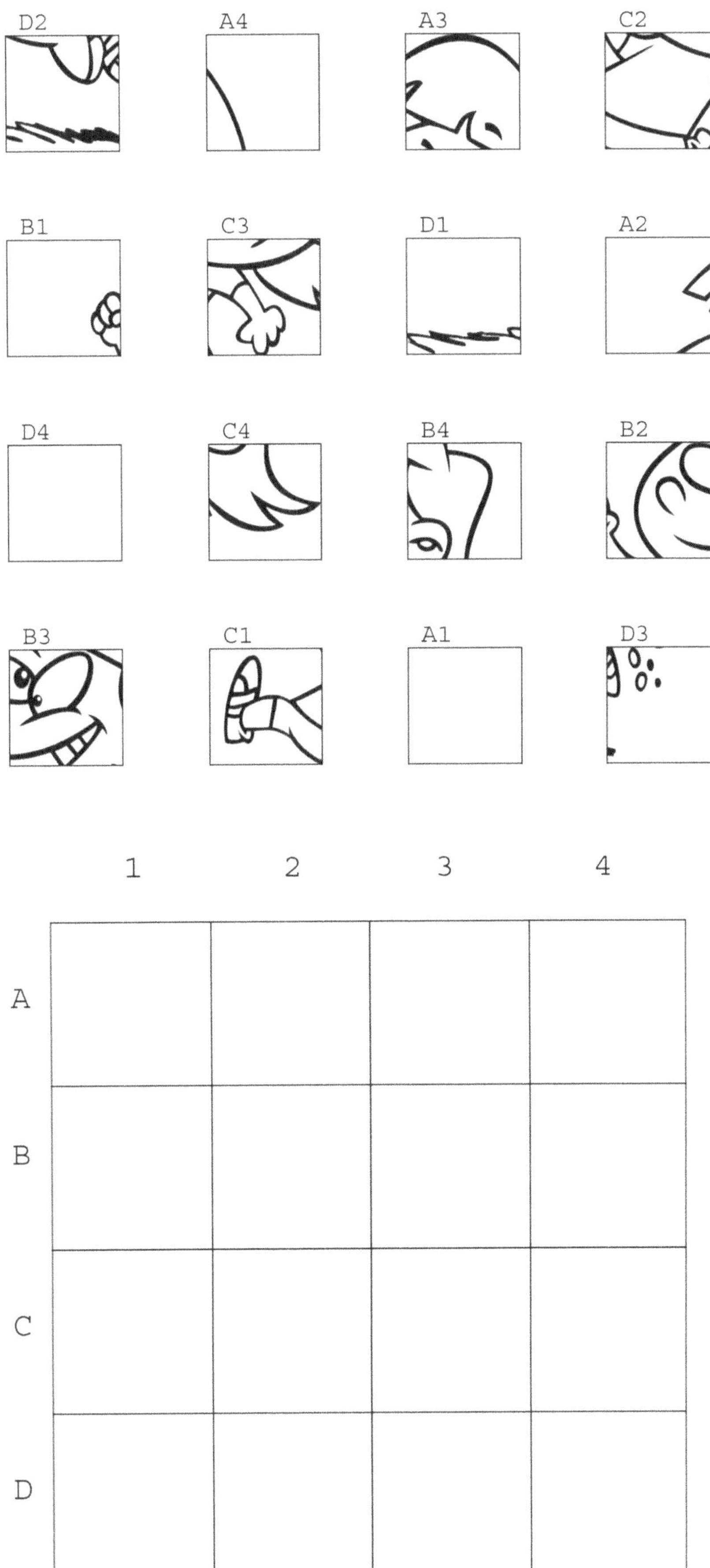

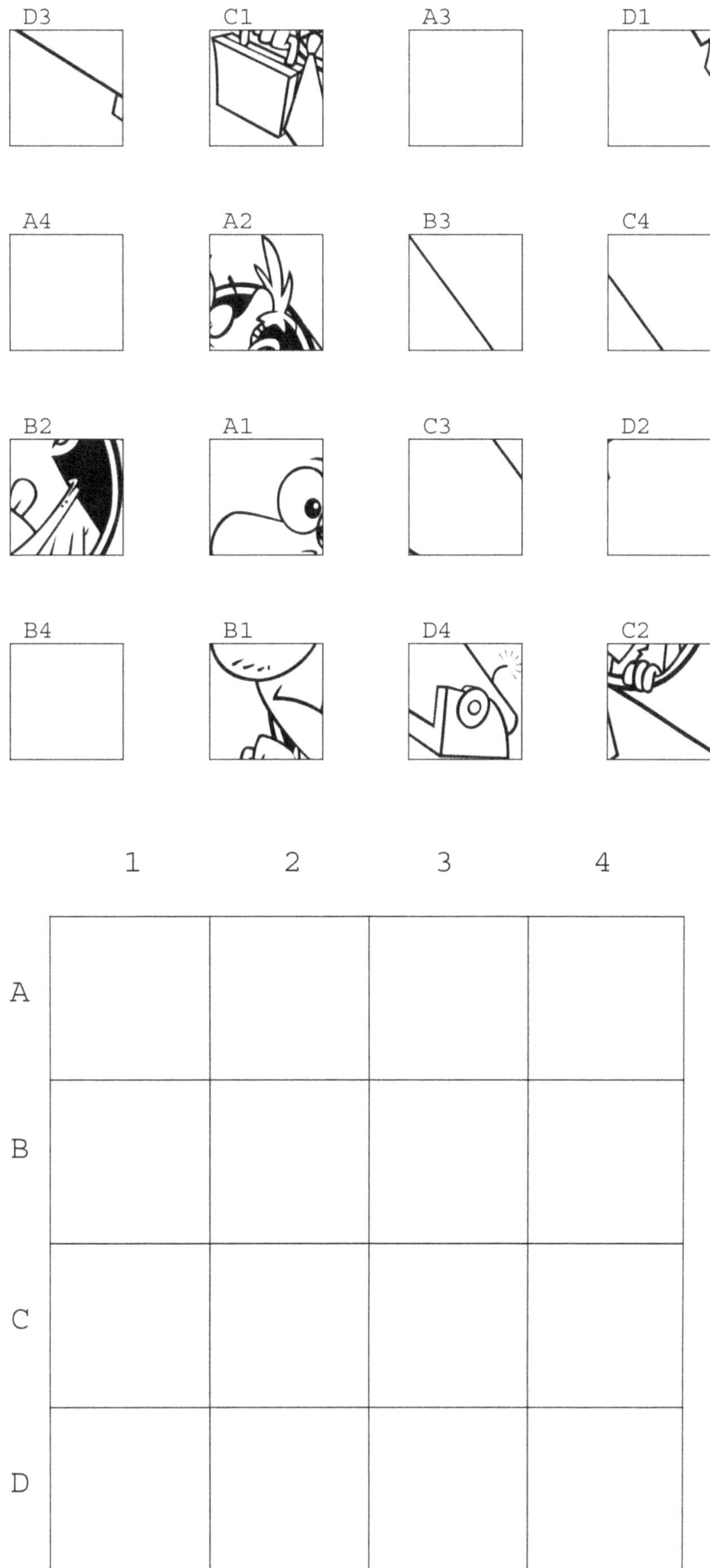

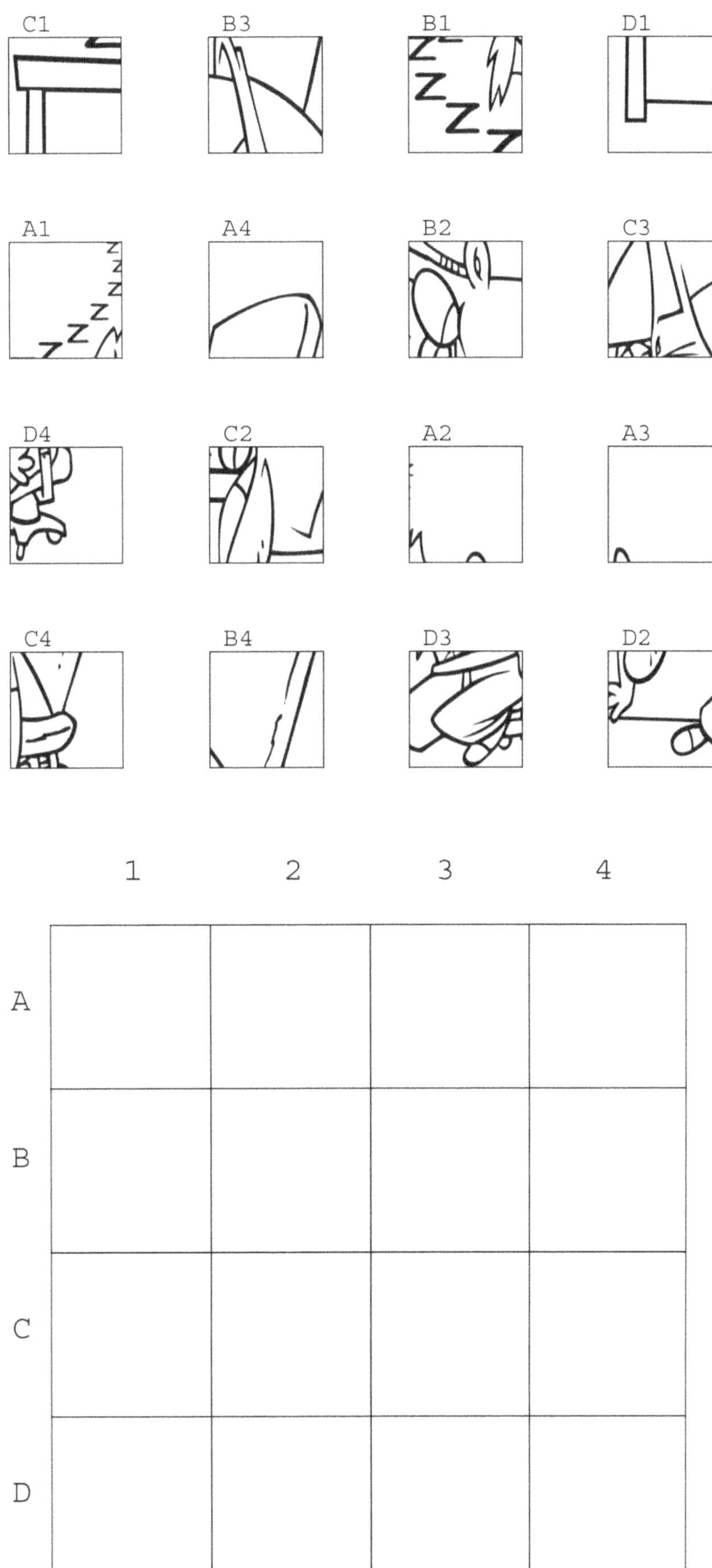

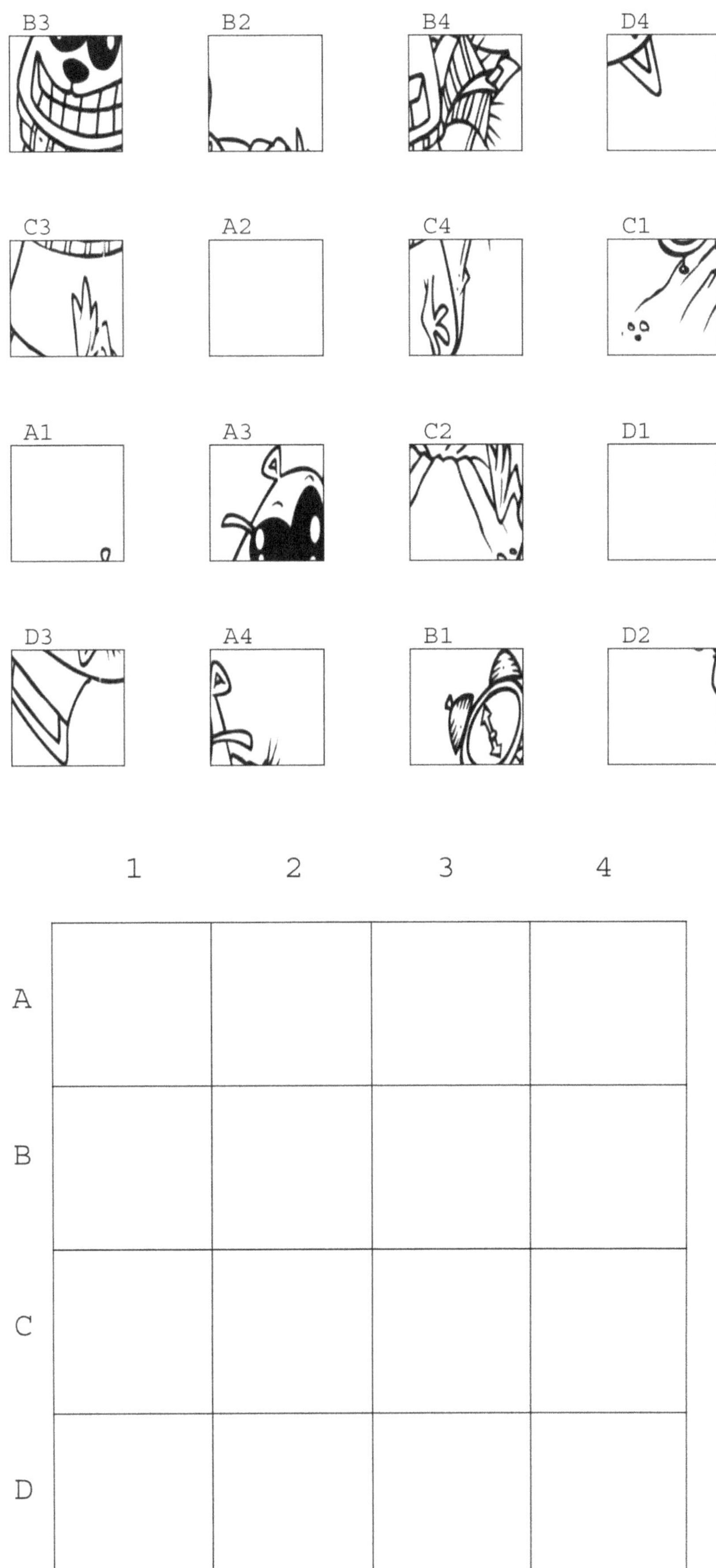

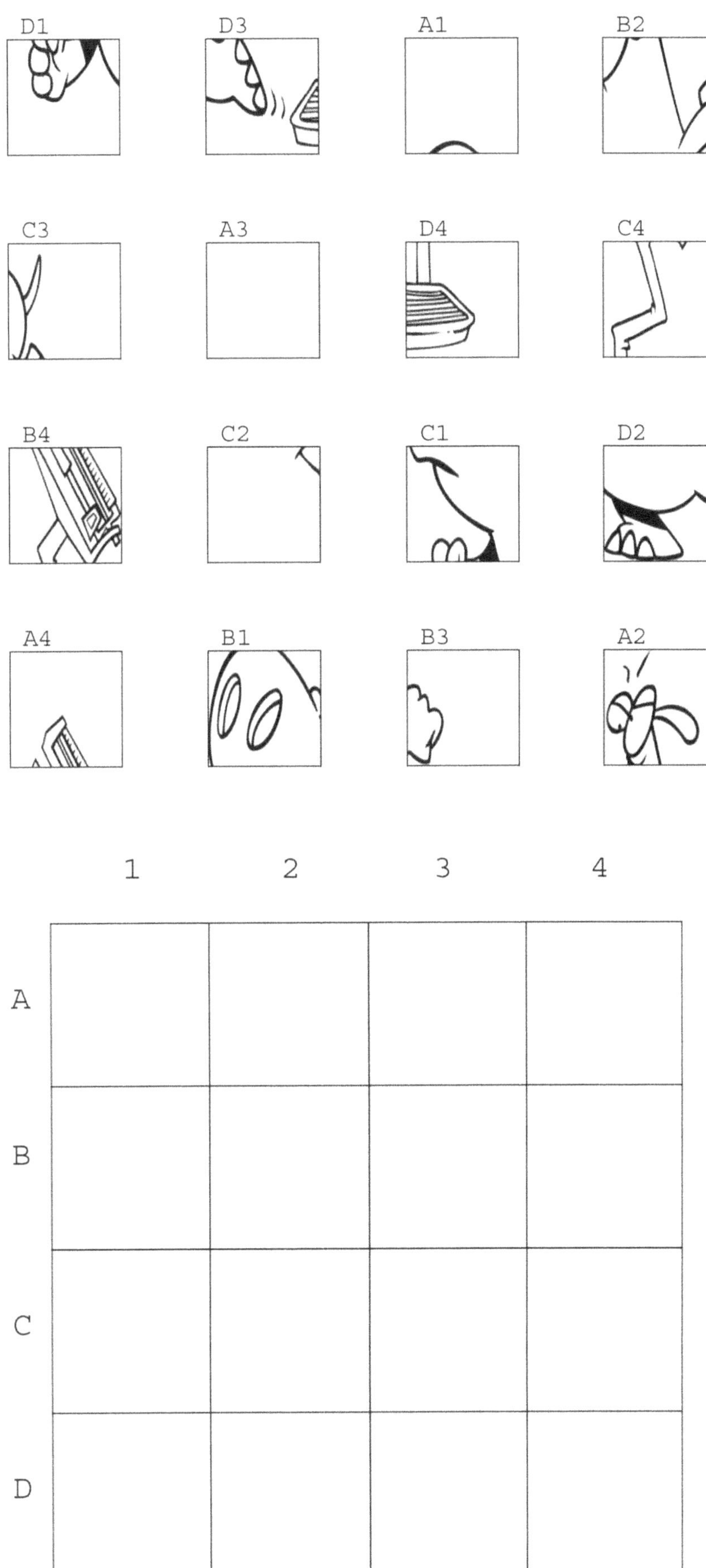

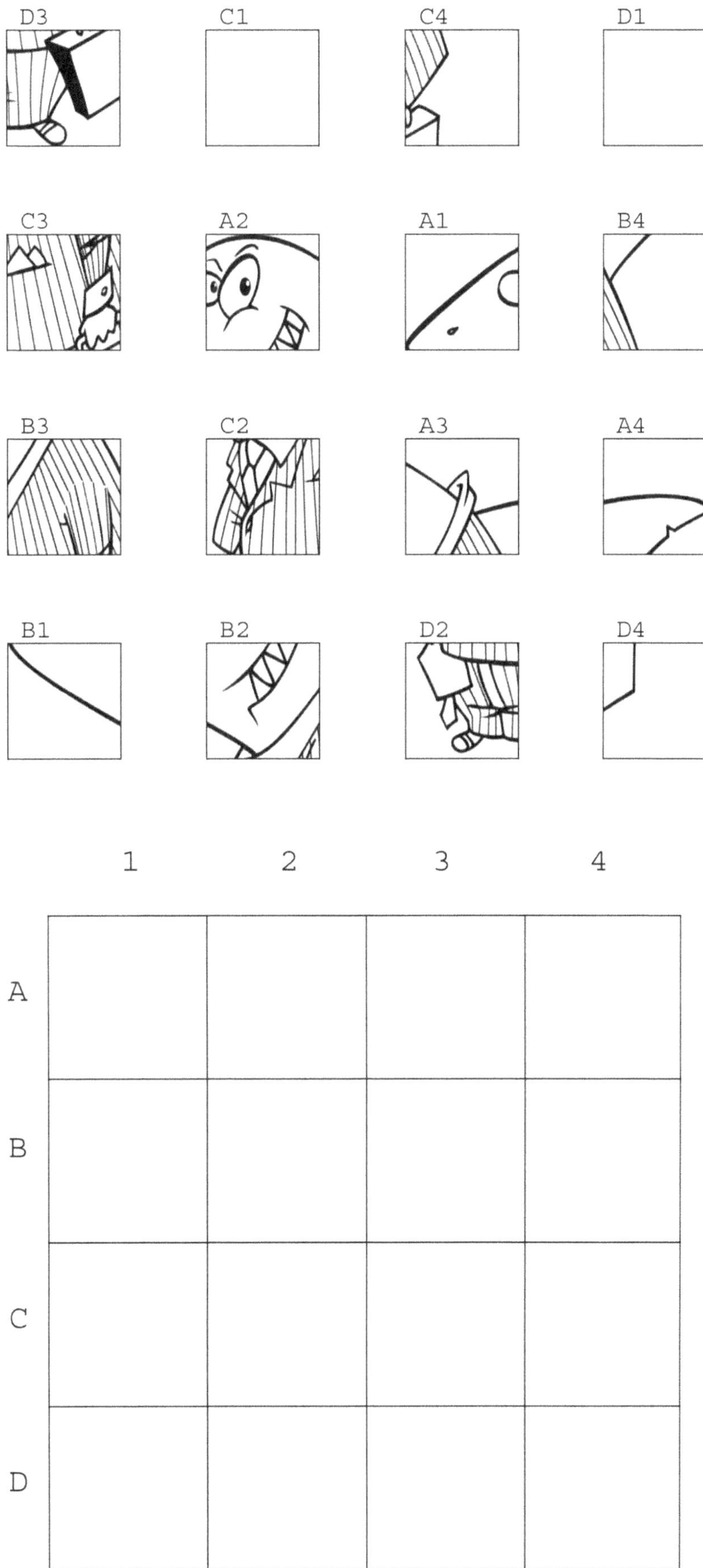

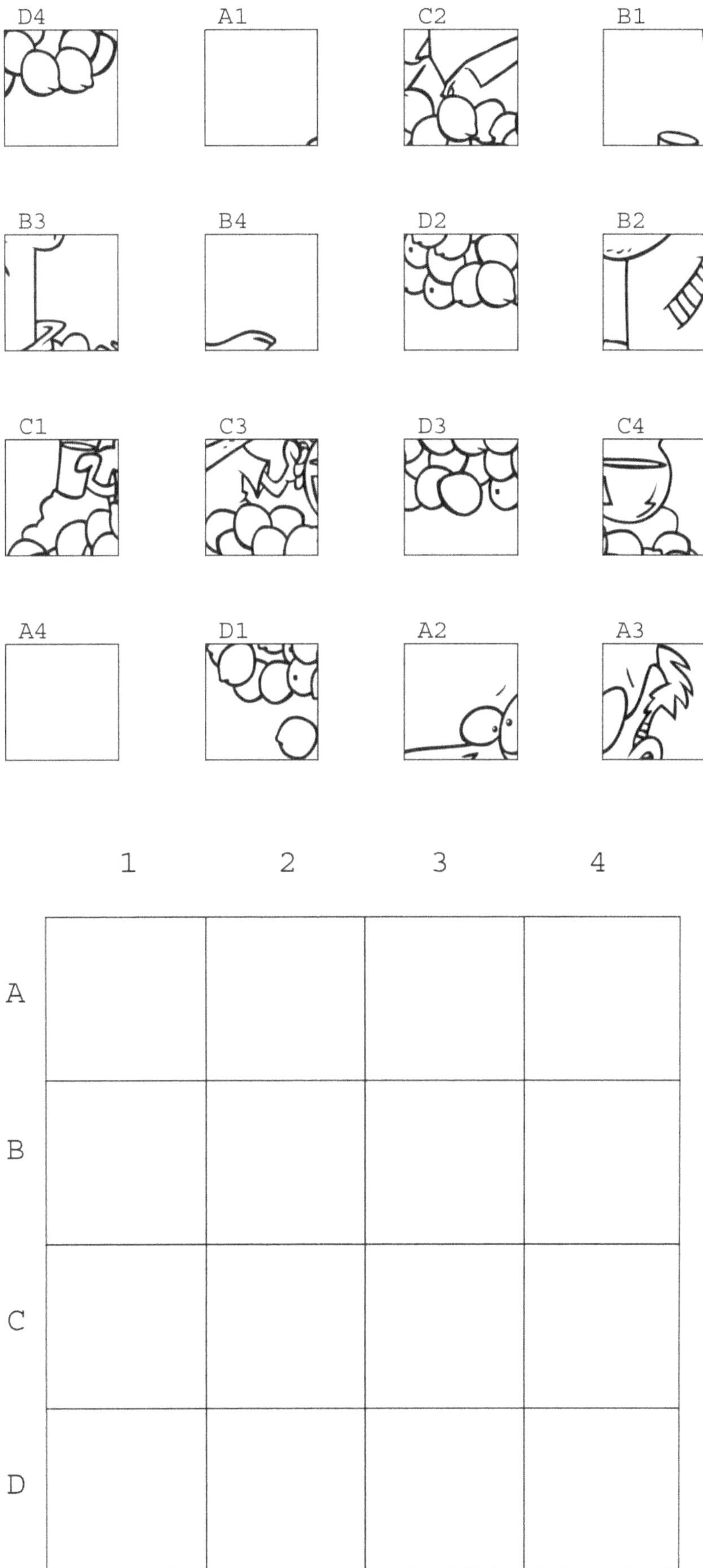

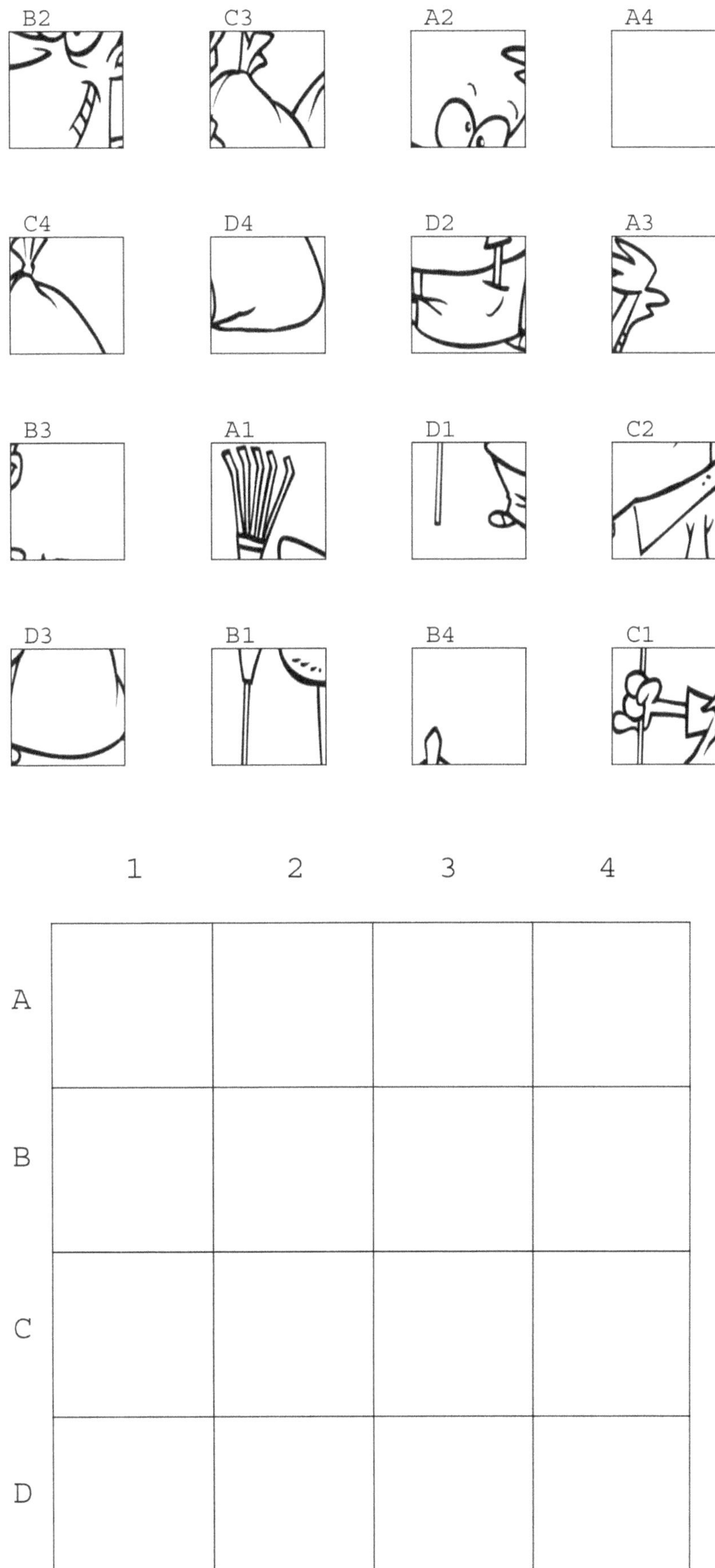

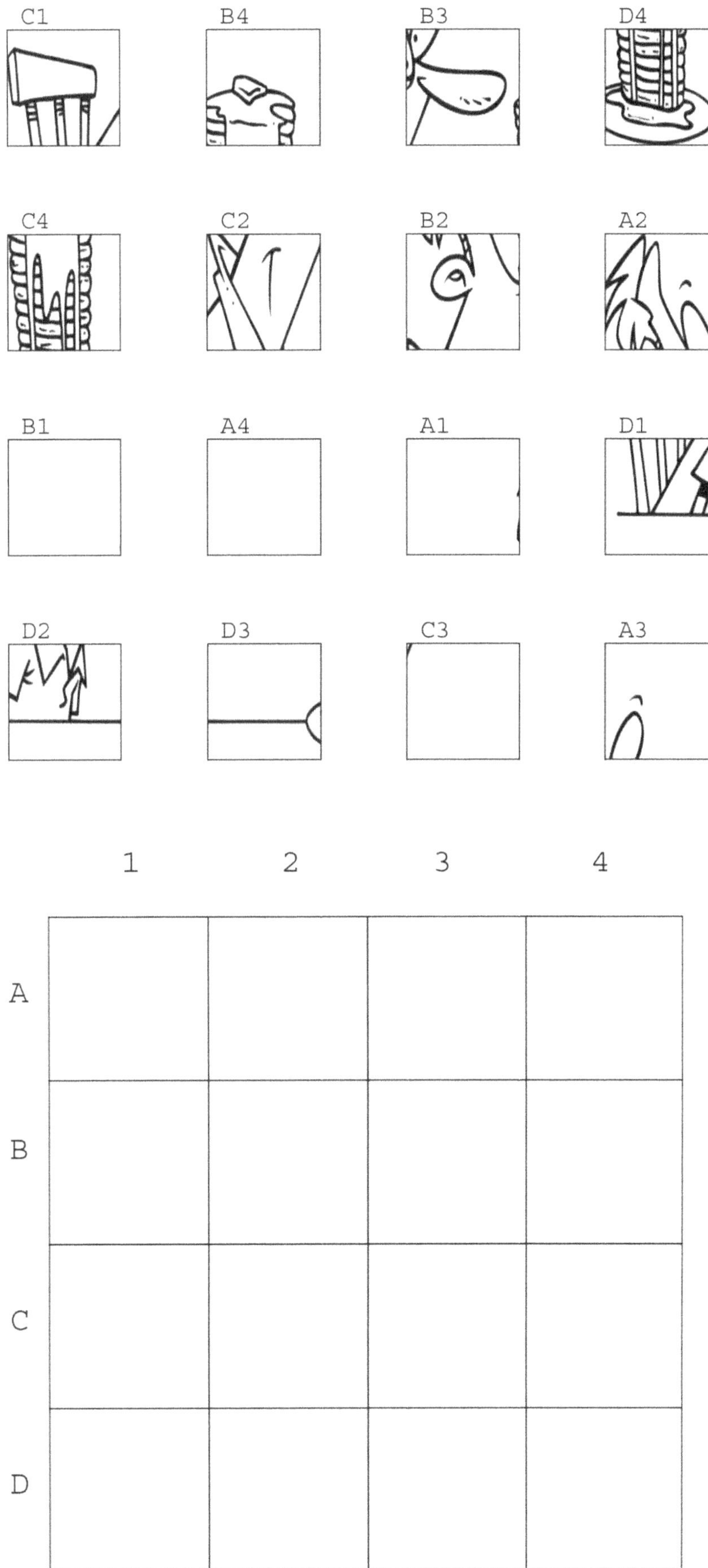

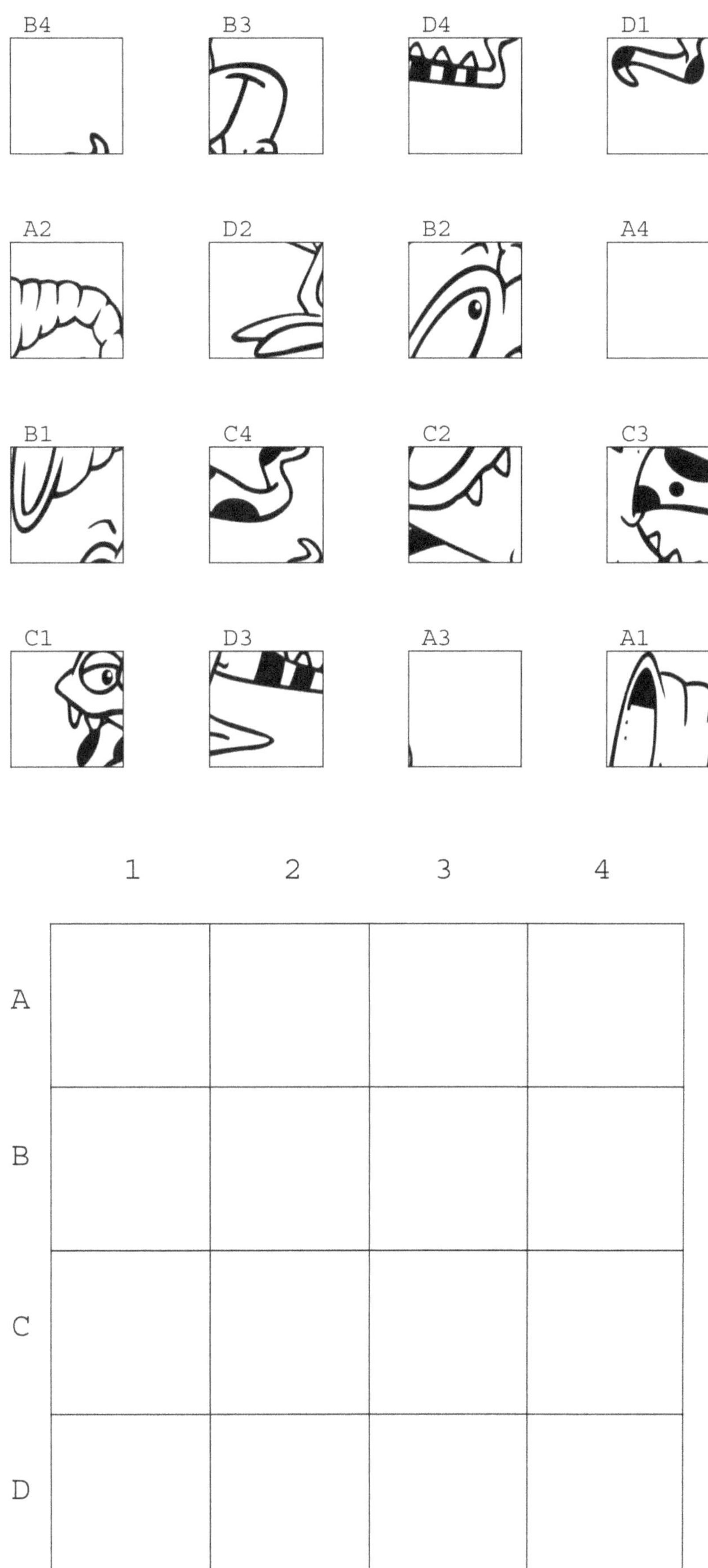

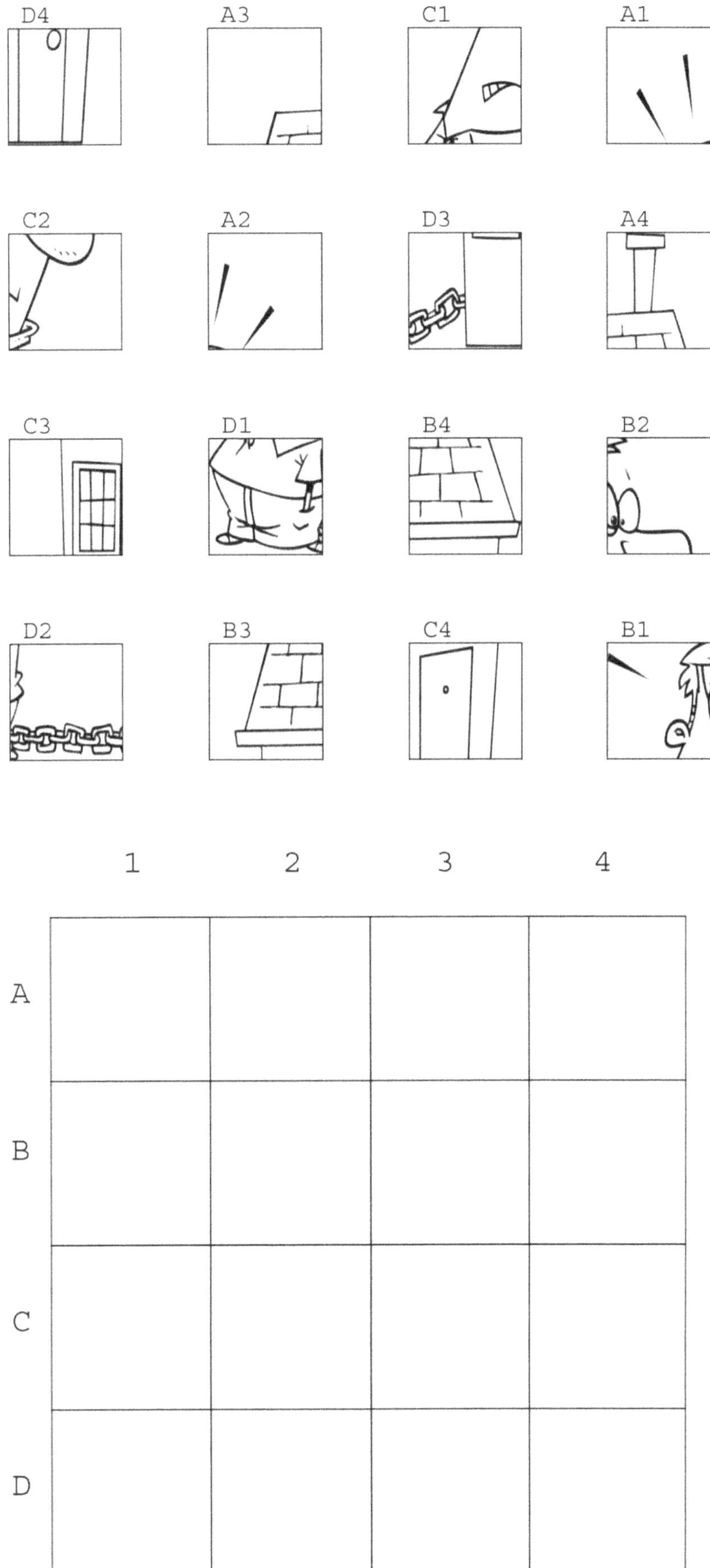

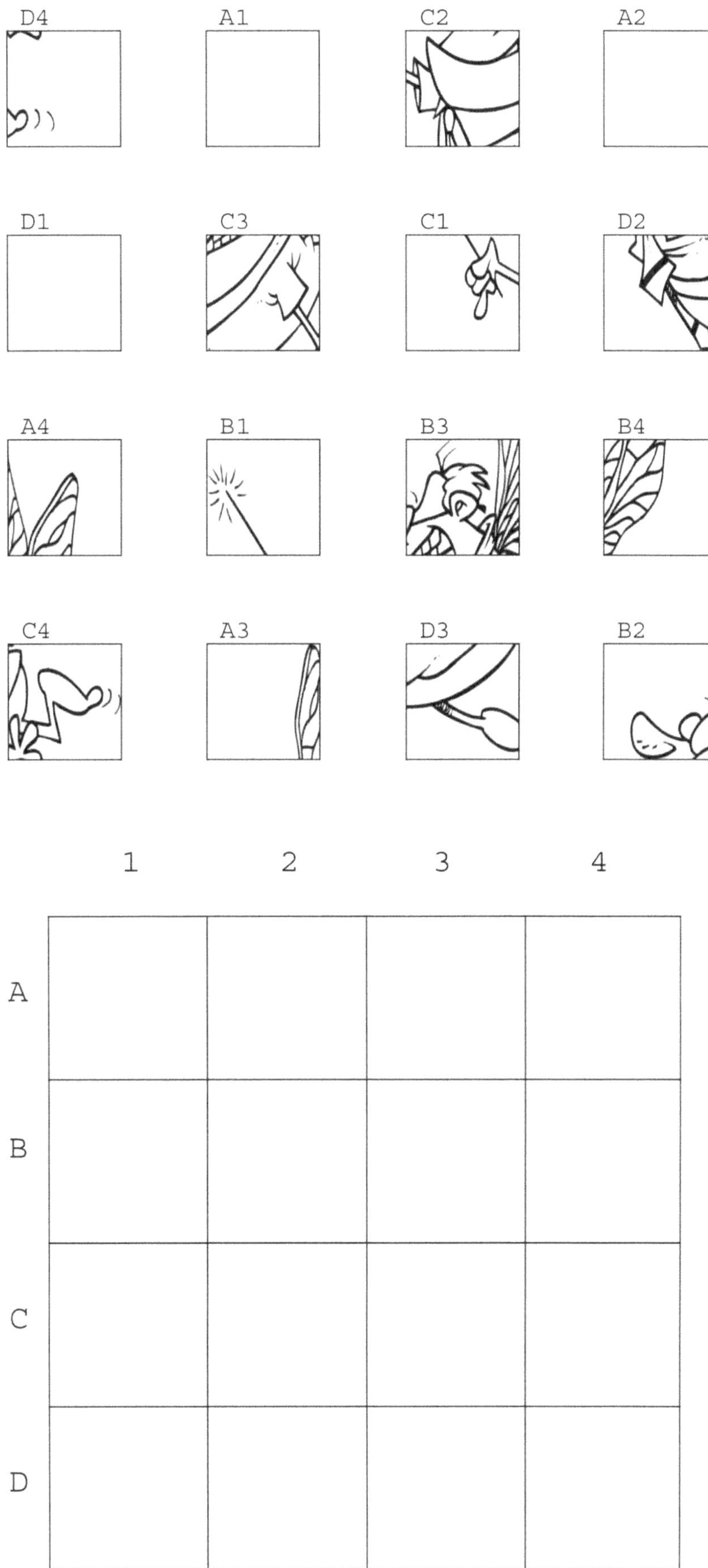

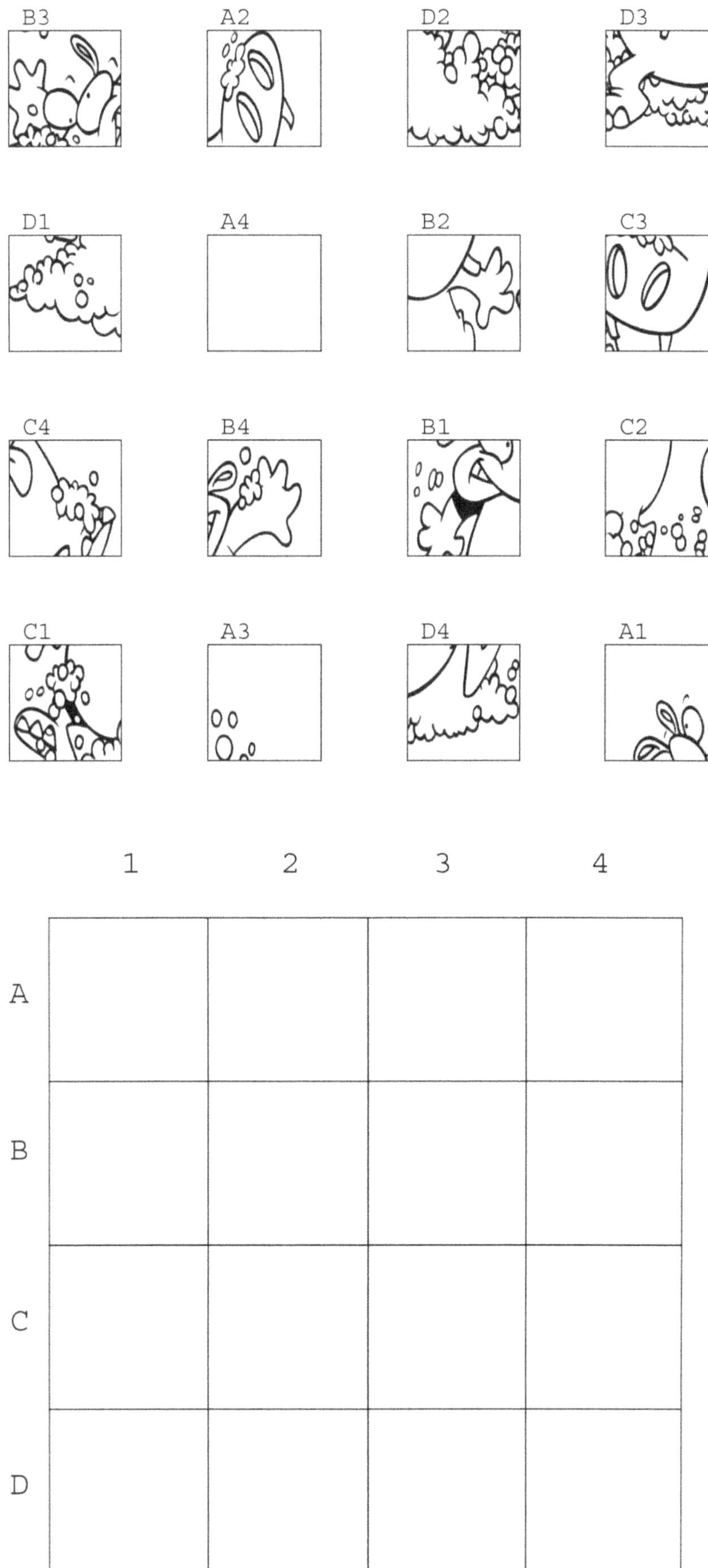

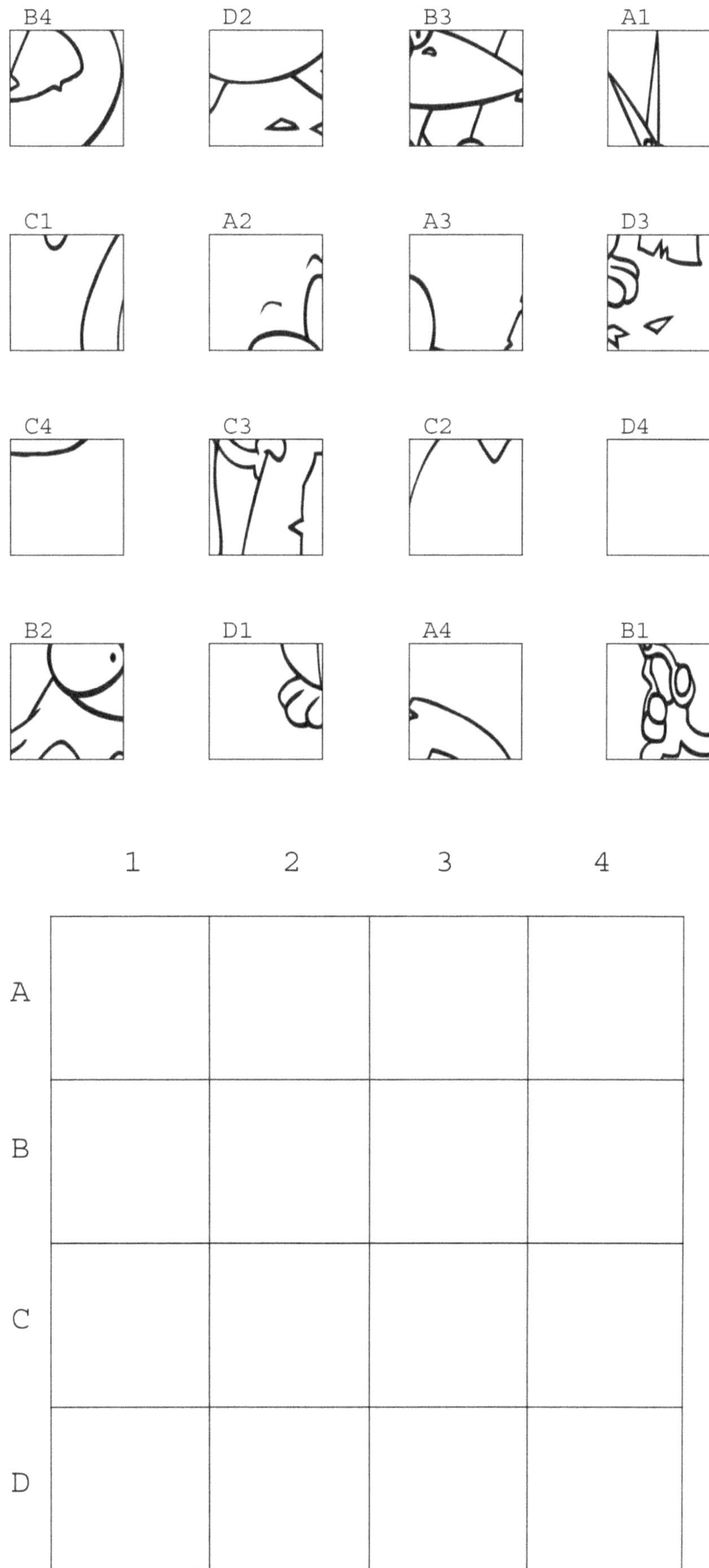

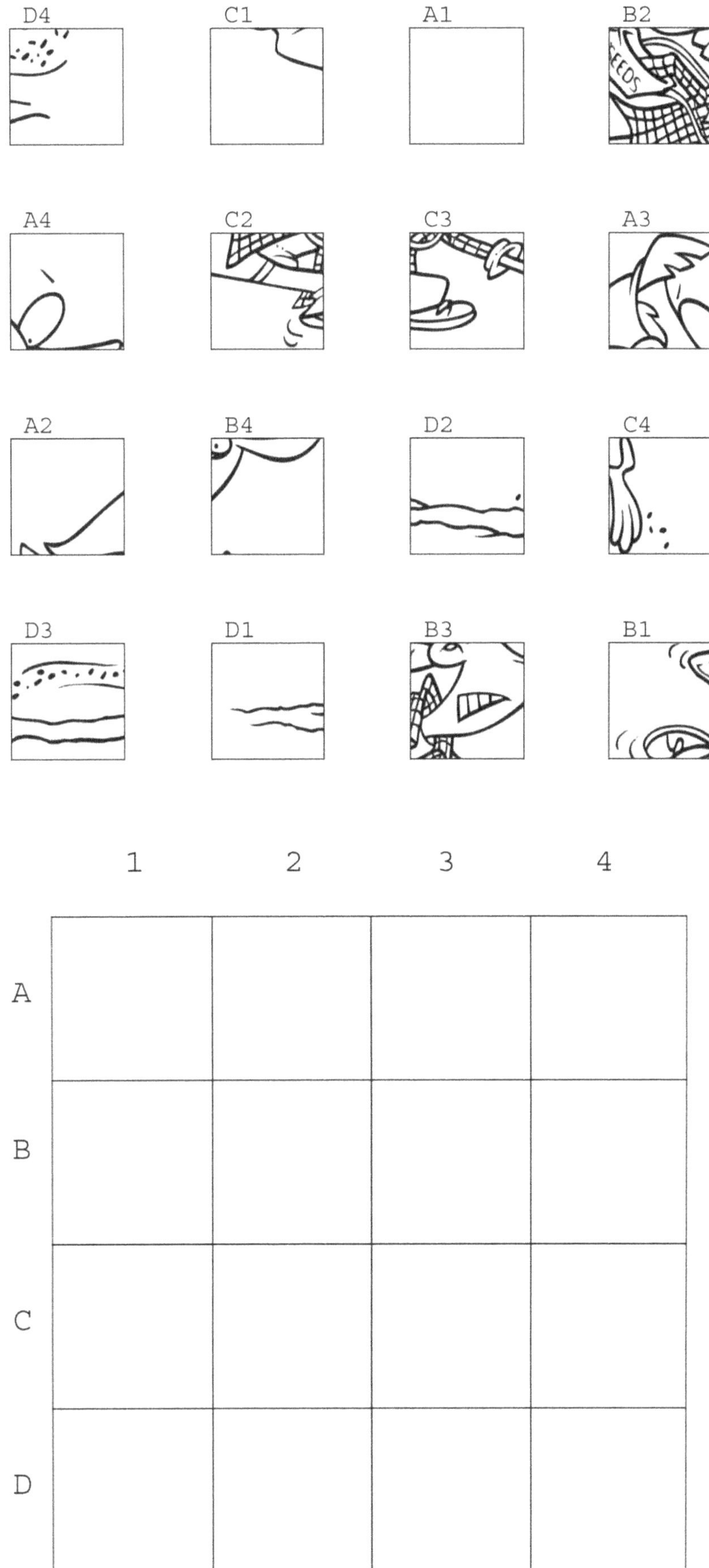

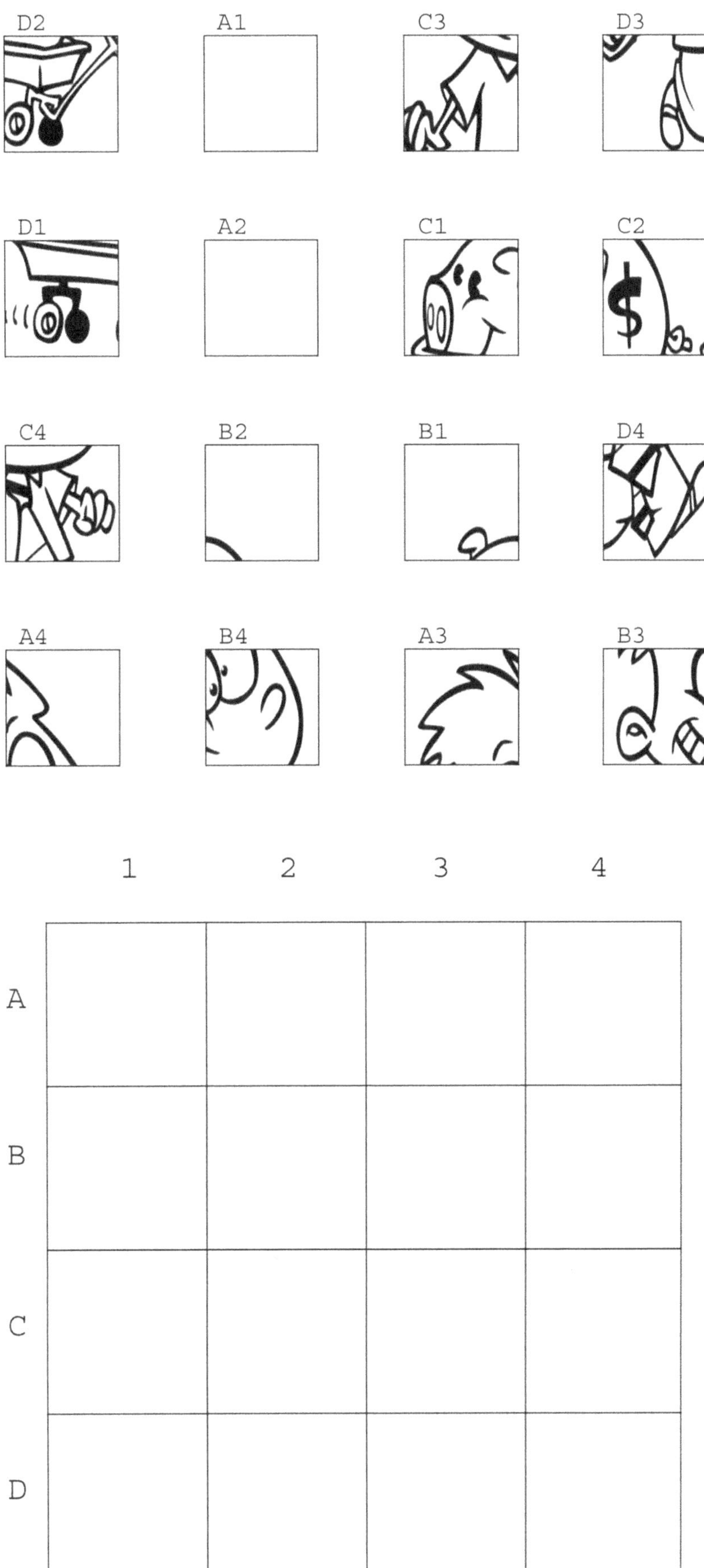

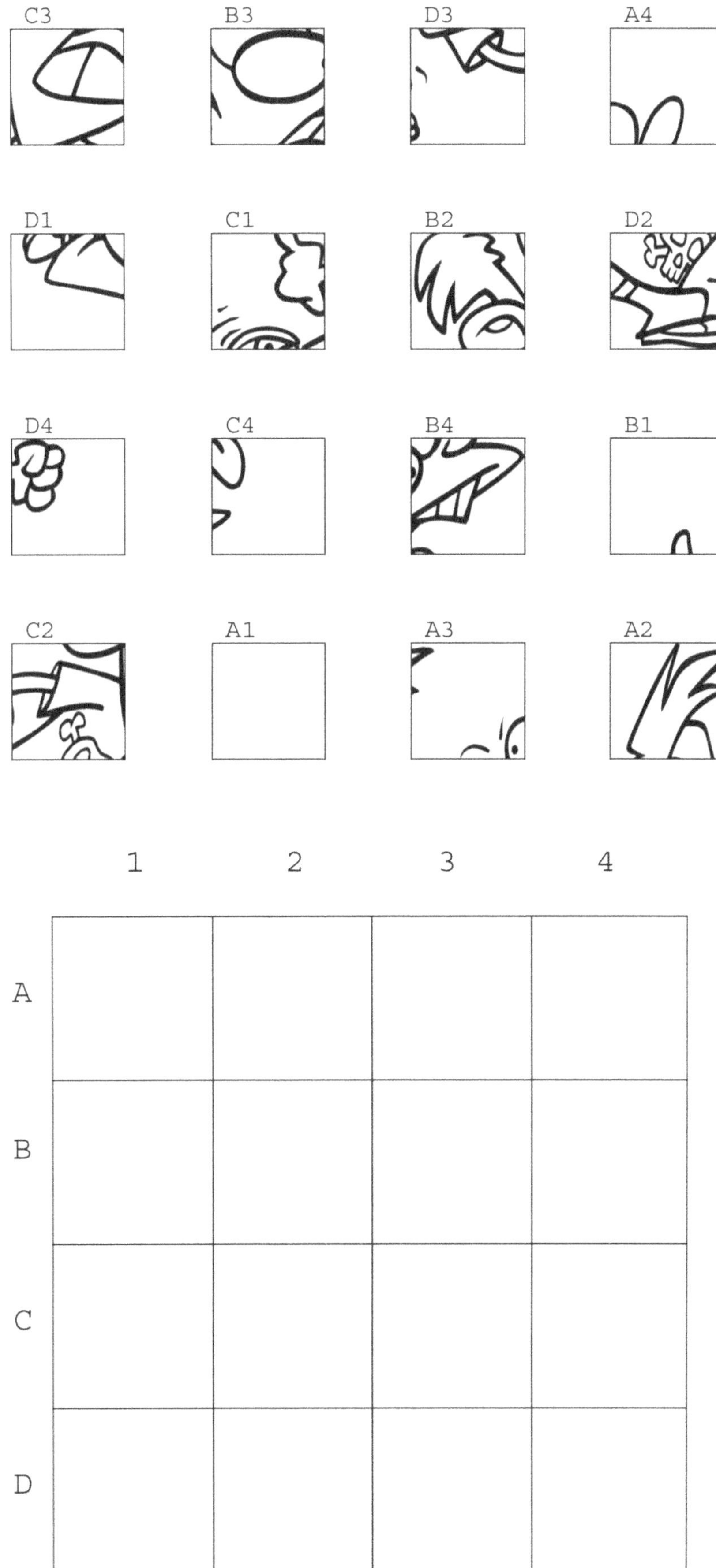

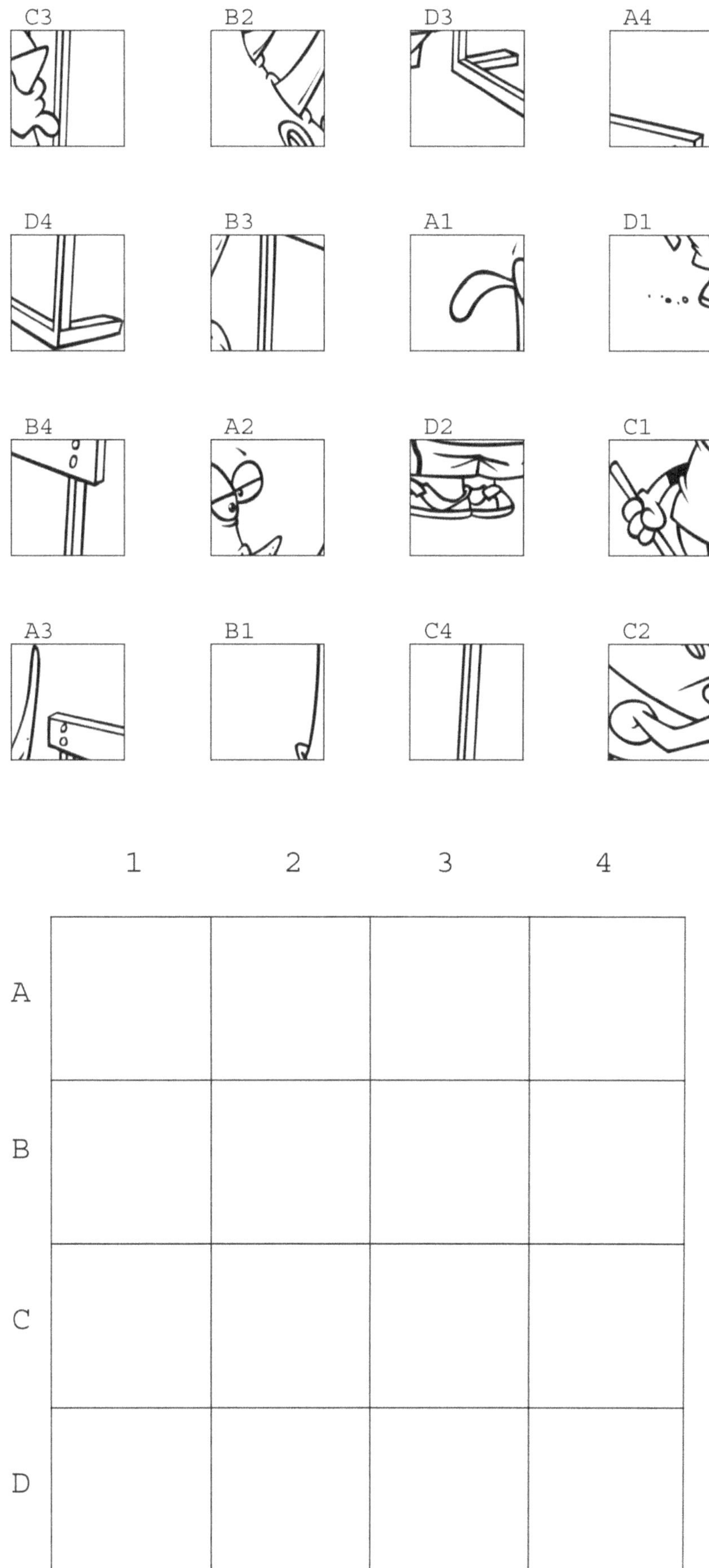

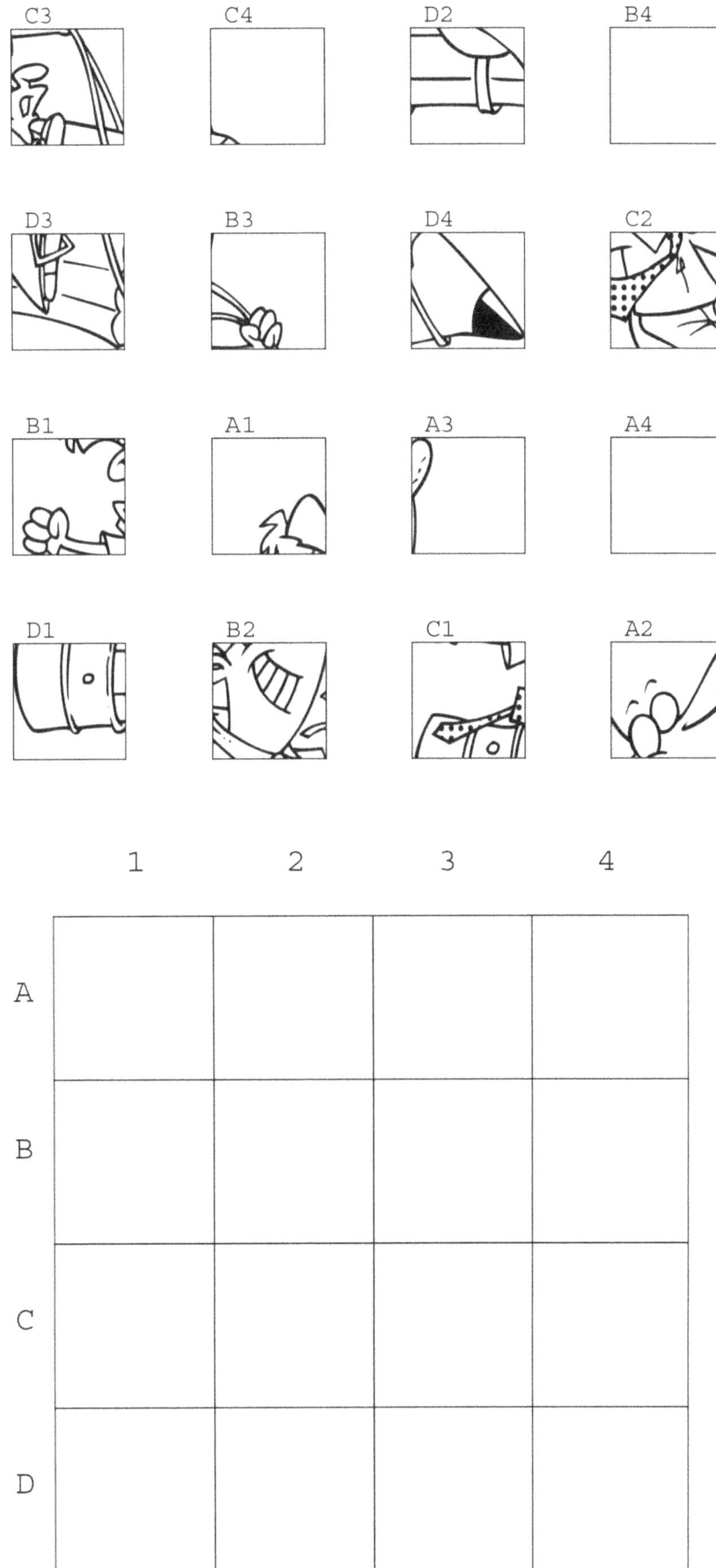

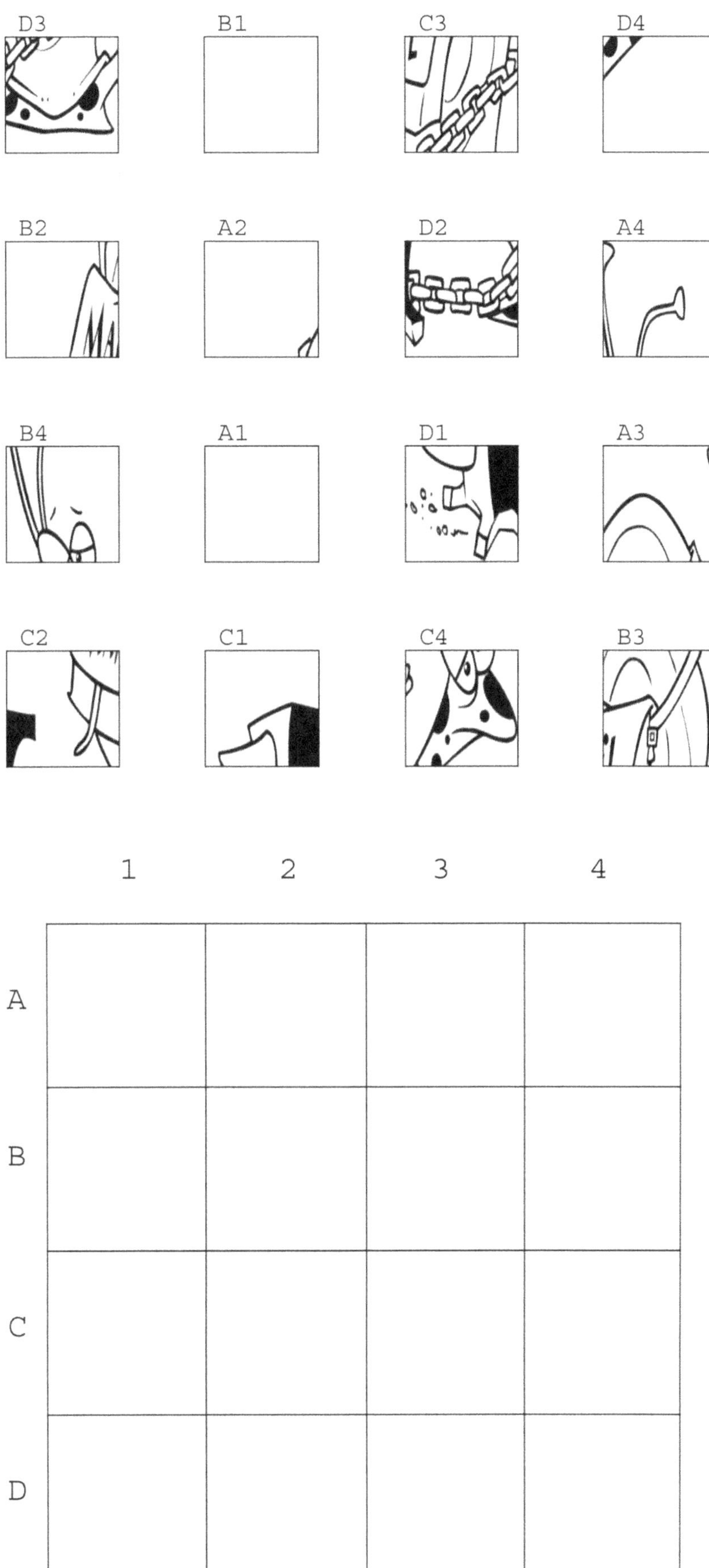

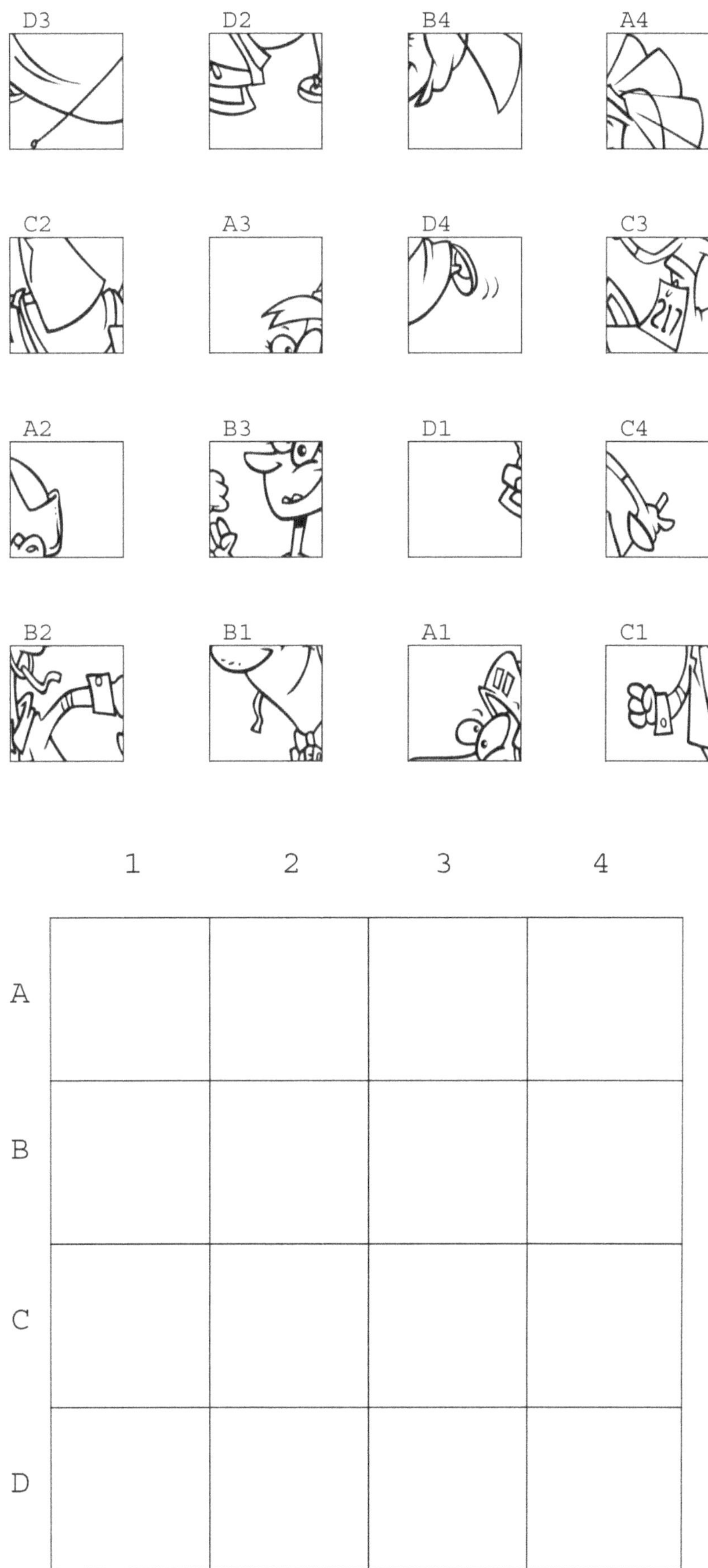

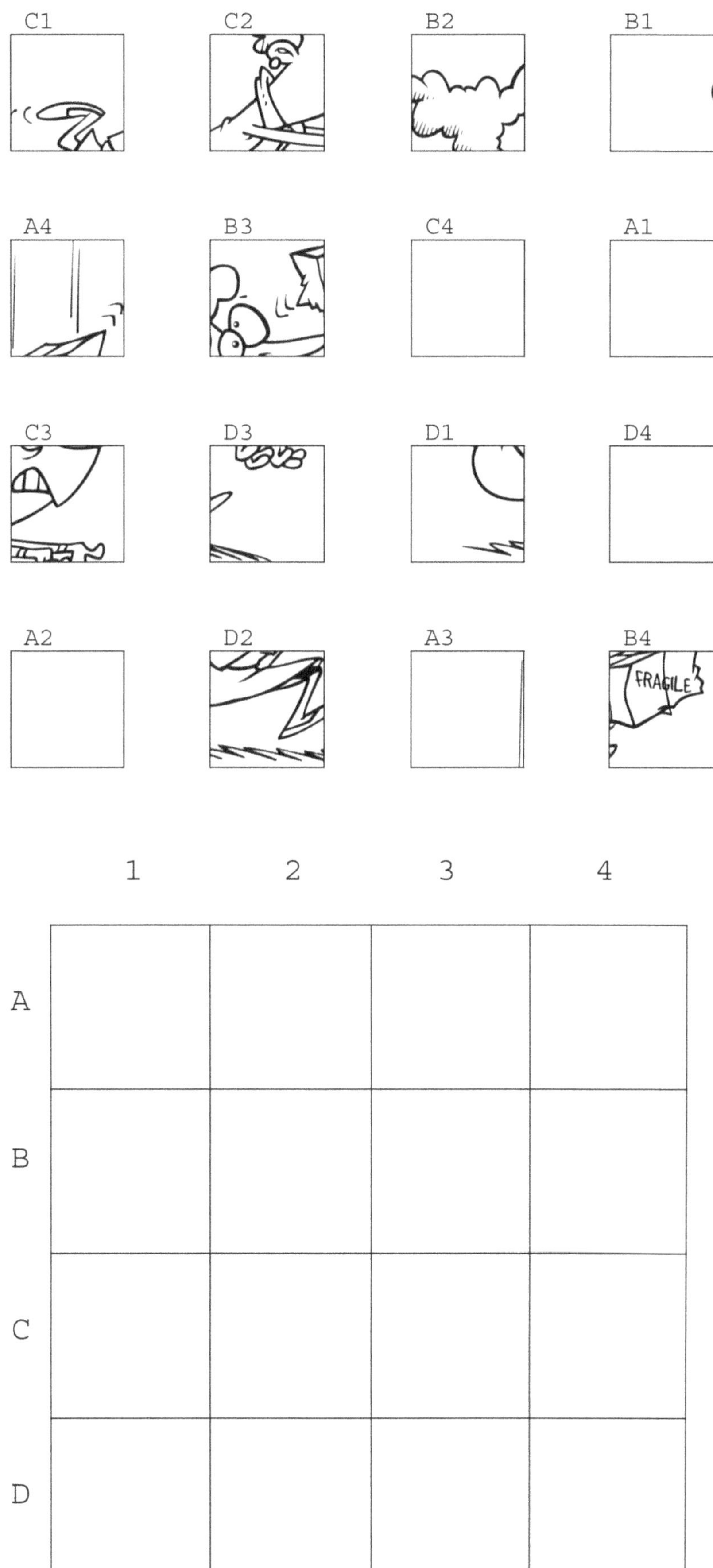

C1
C2
B2
B1
A4
B3
C4
A1
C3
D3
D1
D4
A2
D2
A3
B4
FRAGILE
1
2
3
4
A
B
C
D

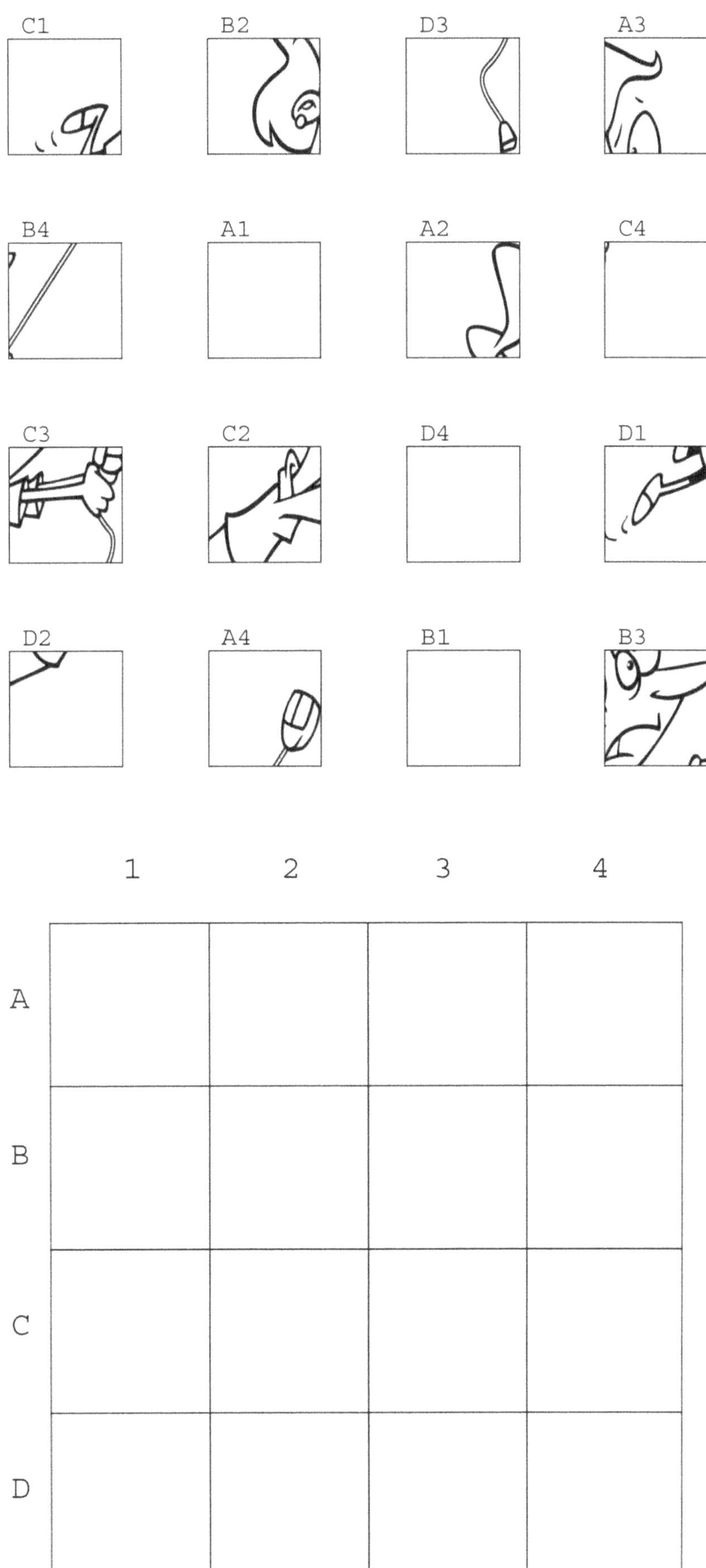

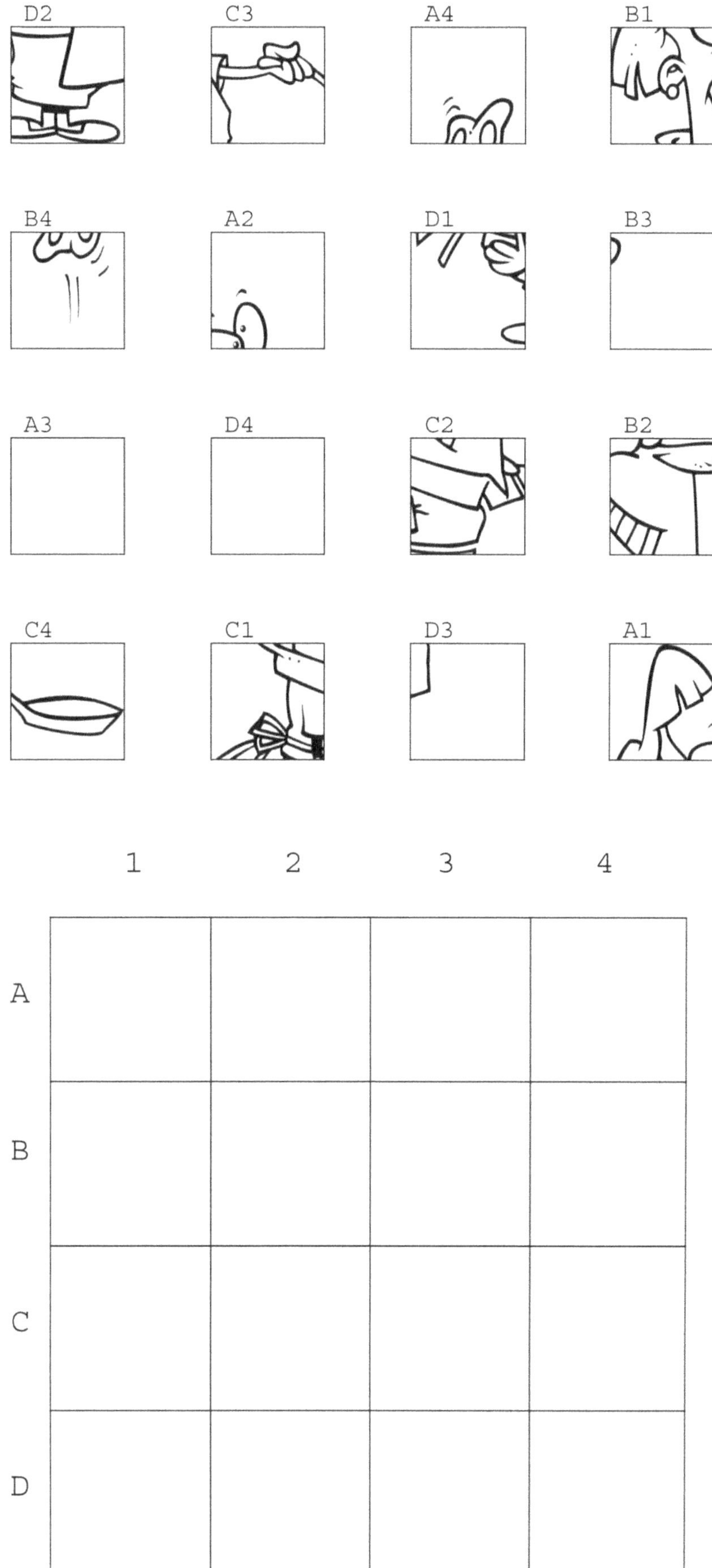

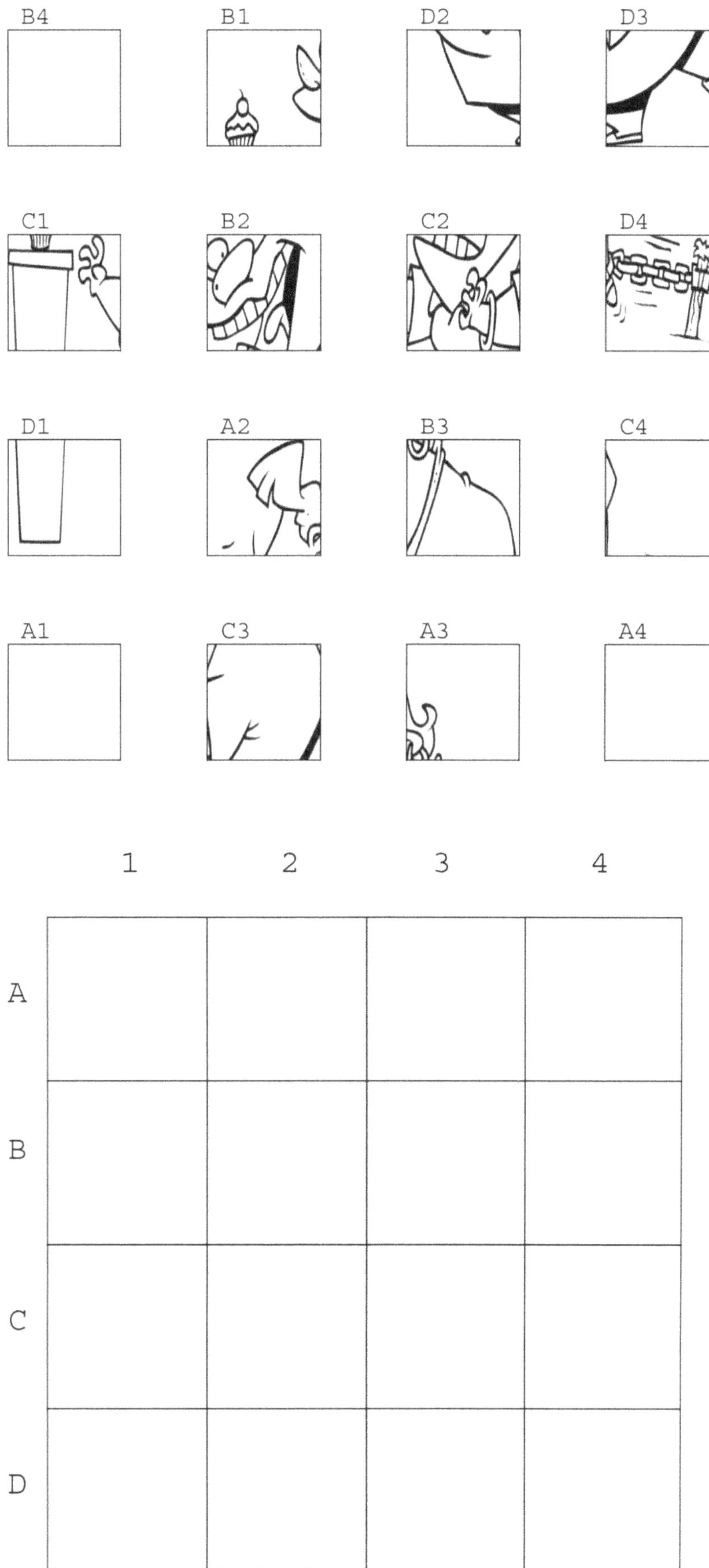

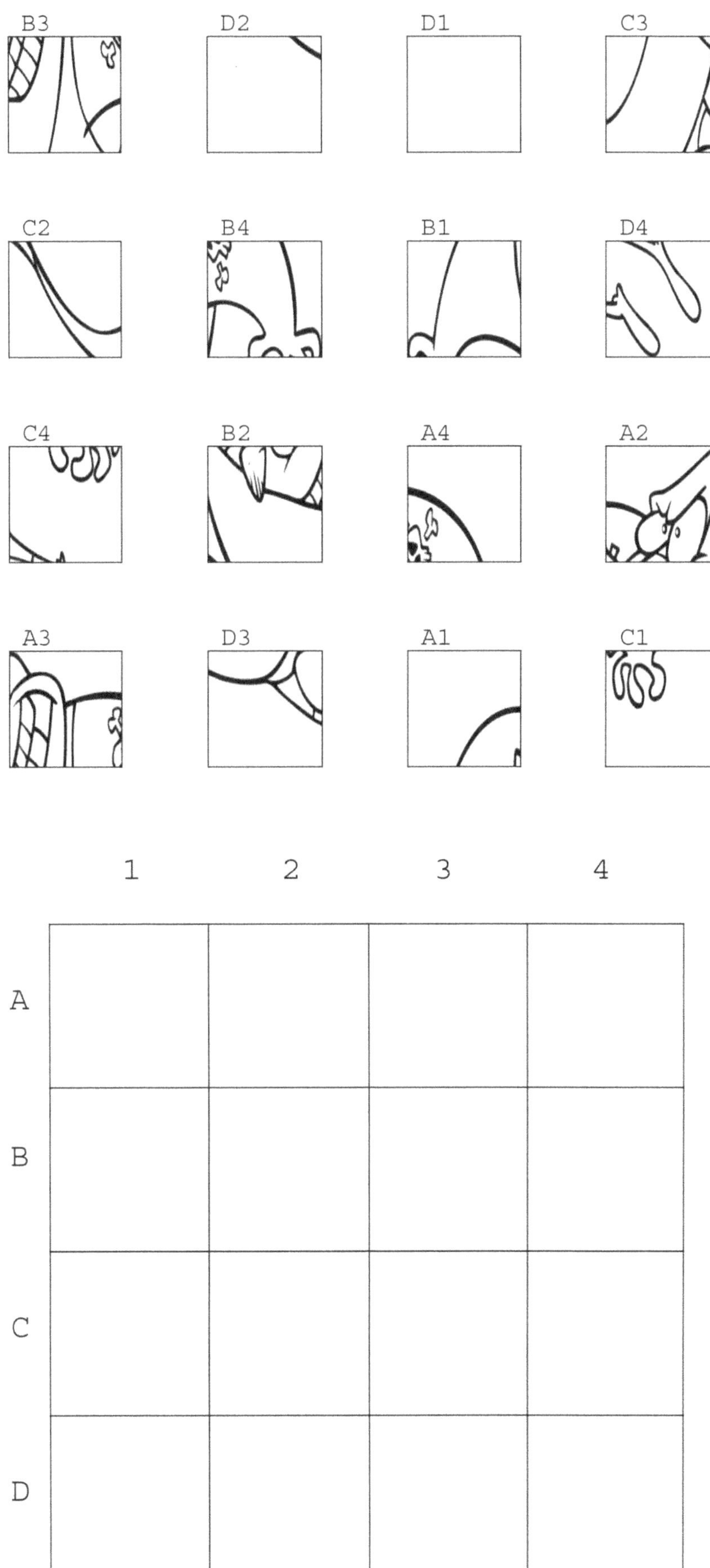

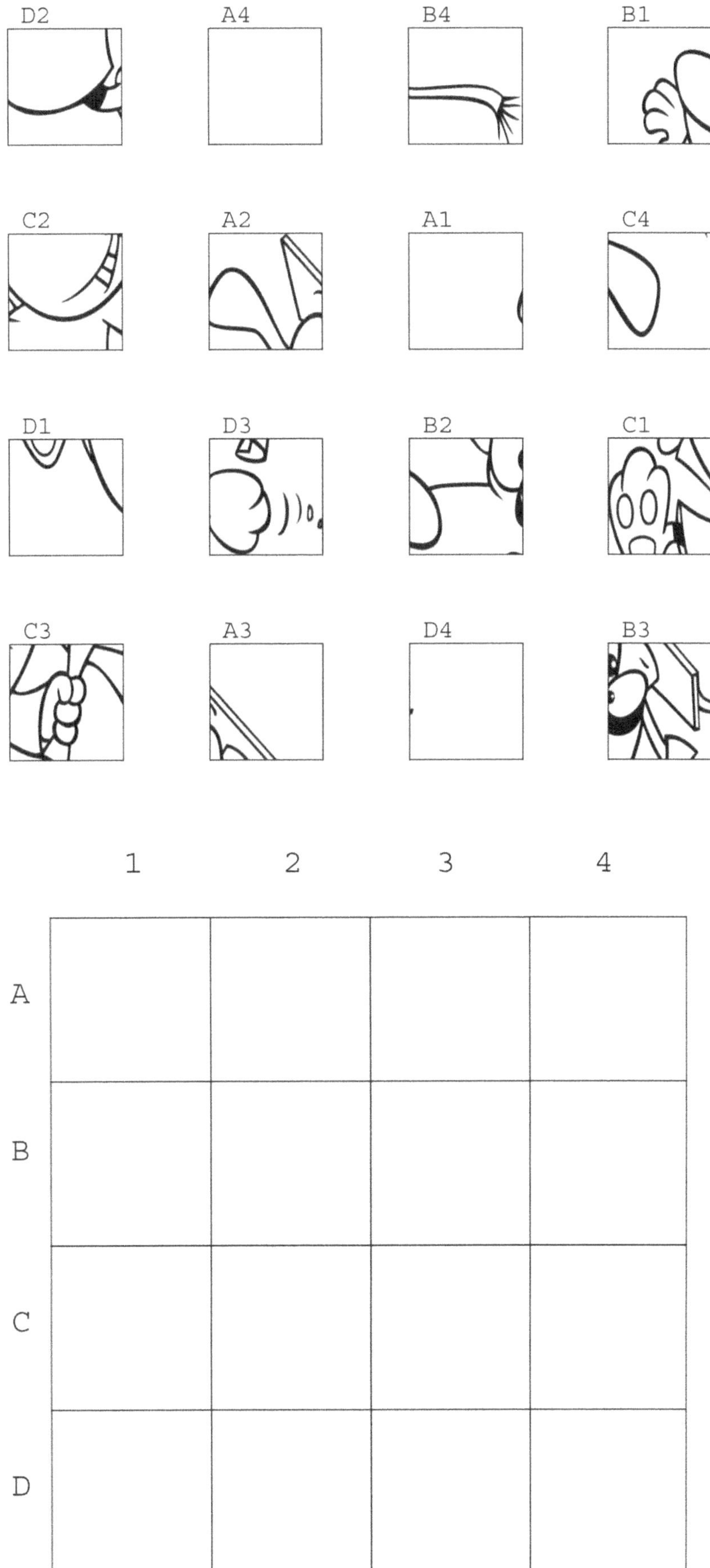

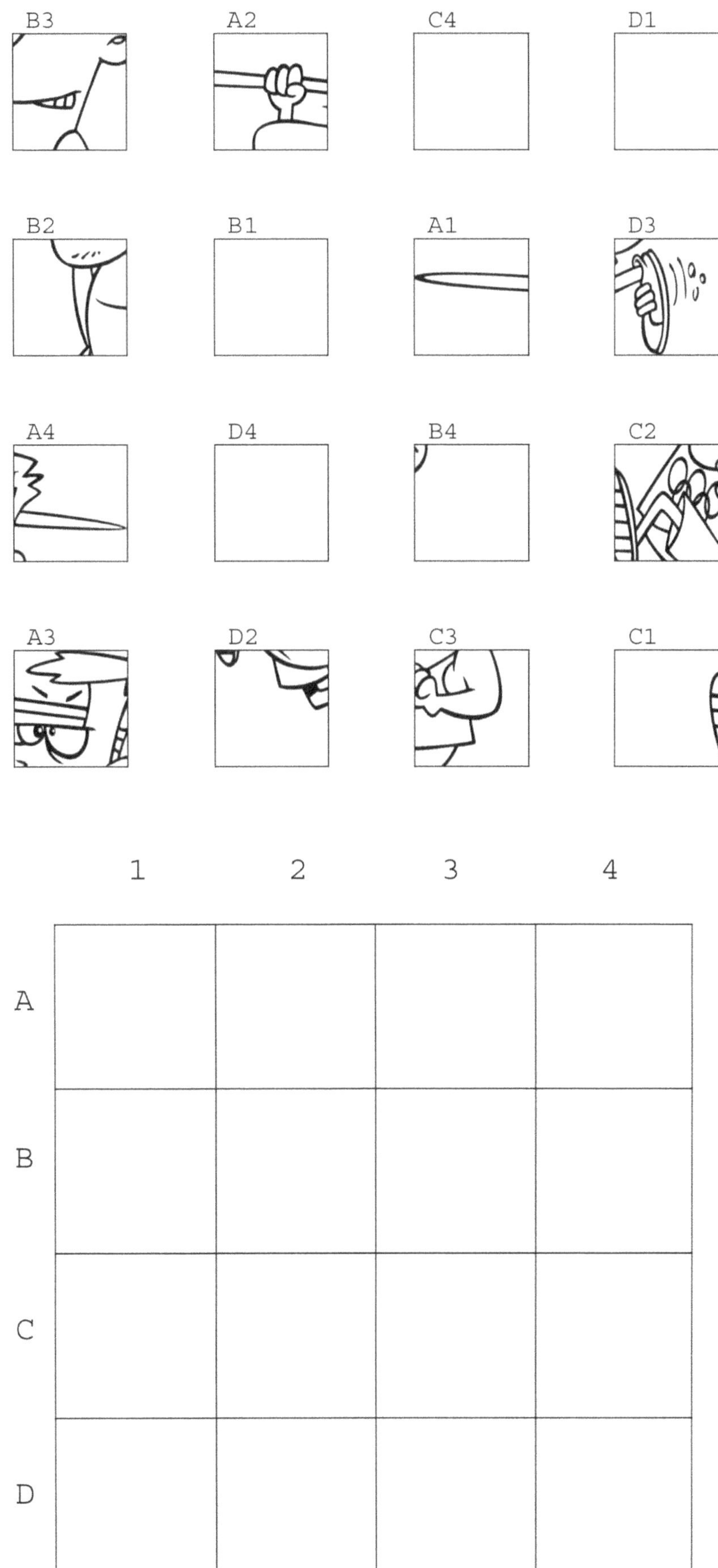

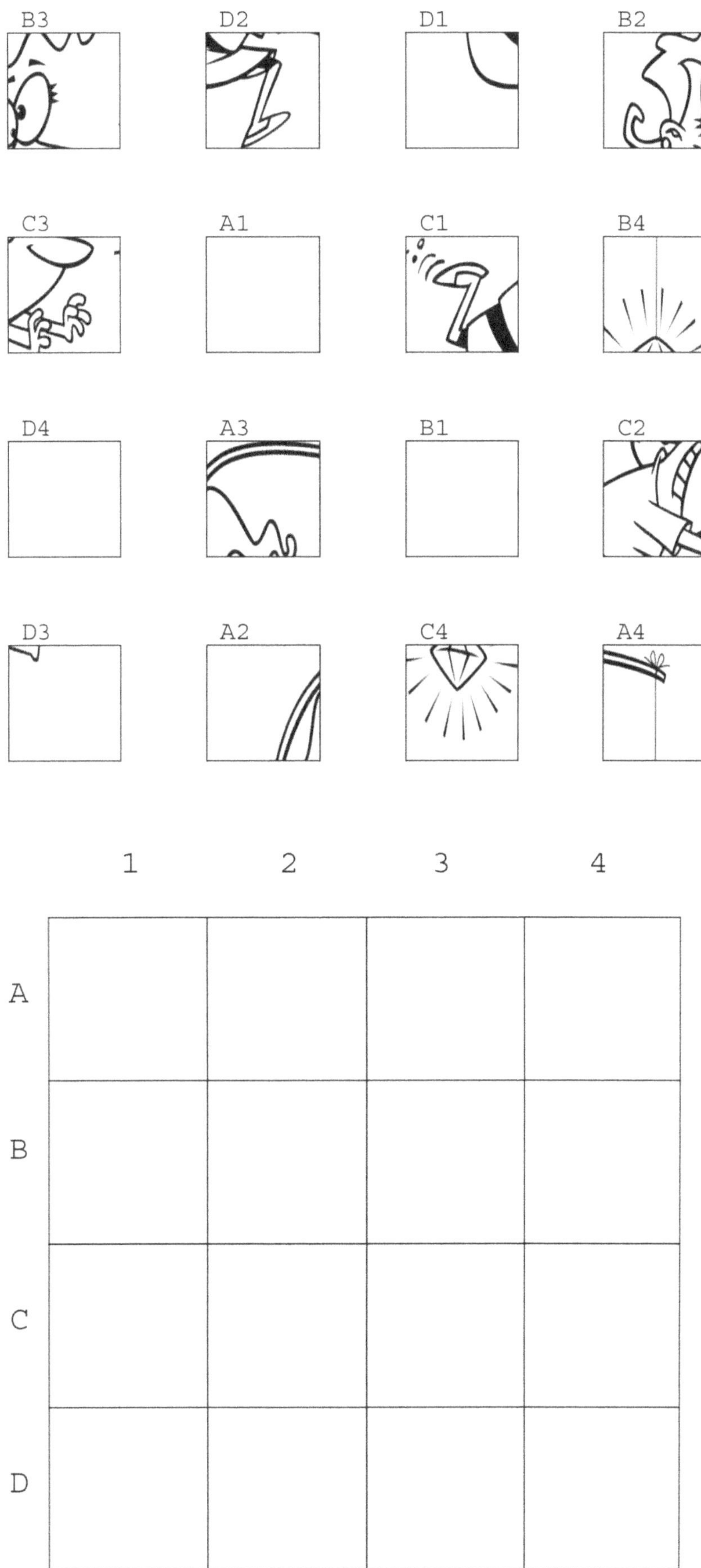

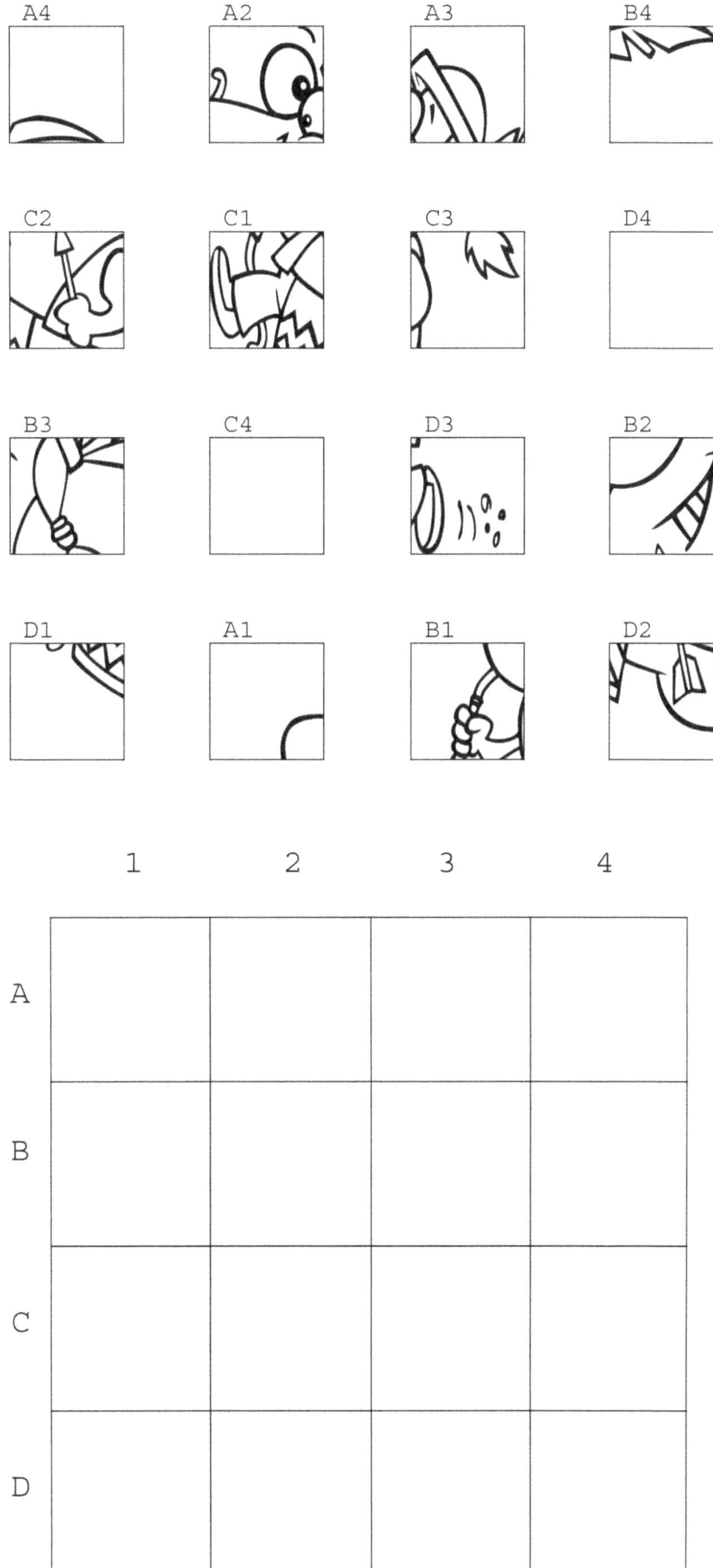

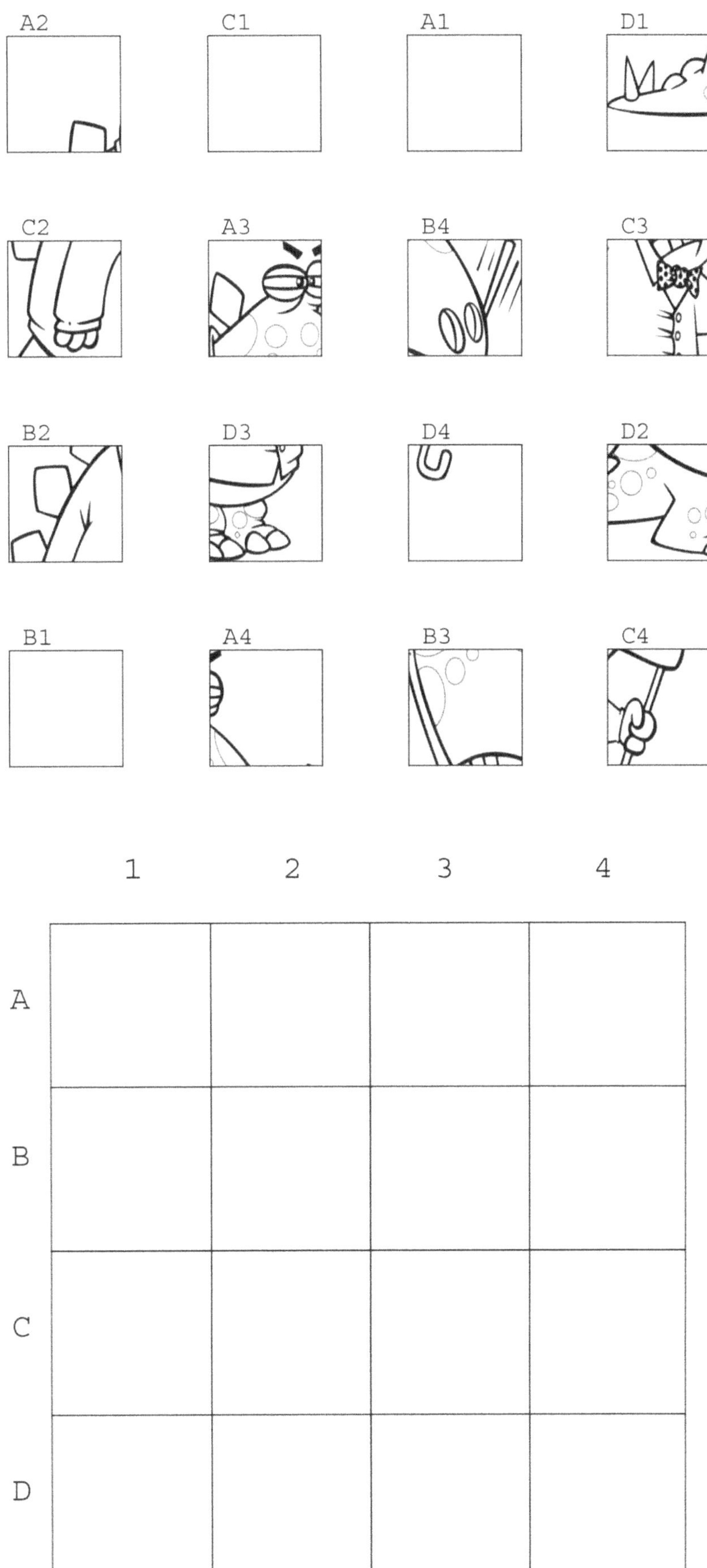

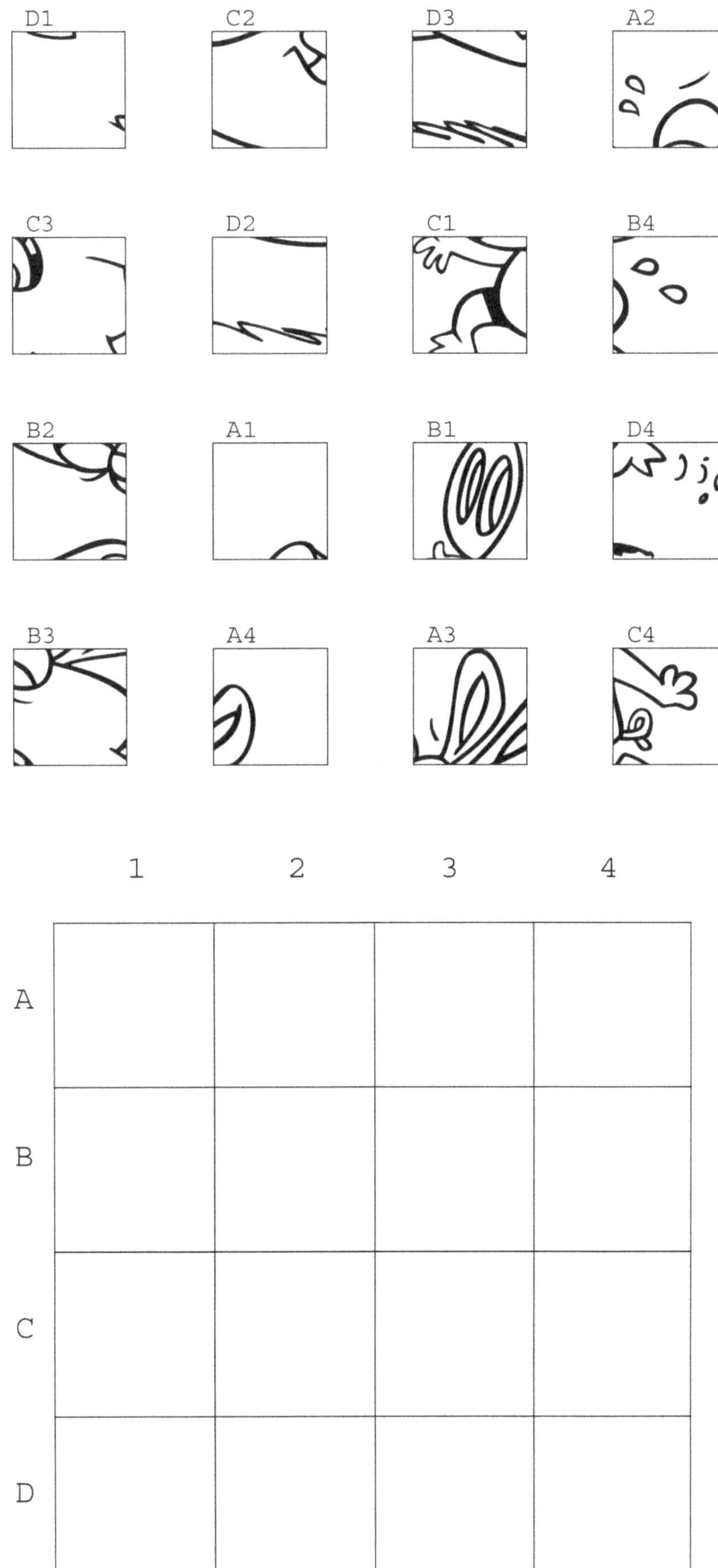

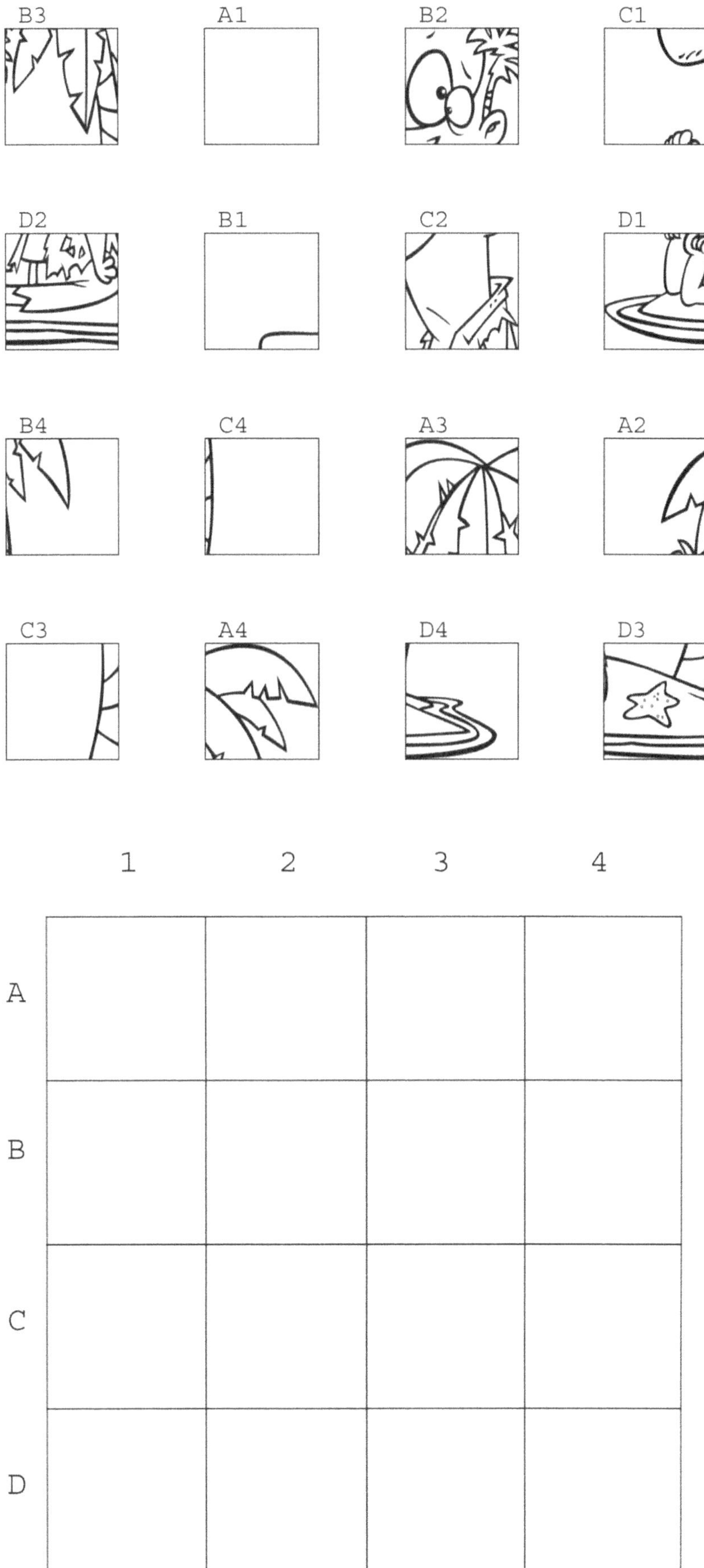

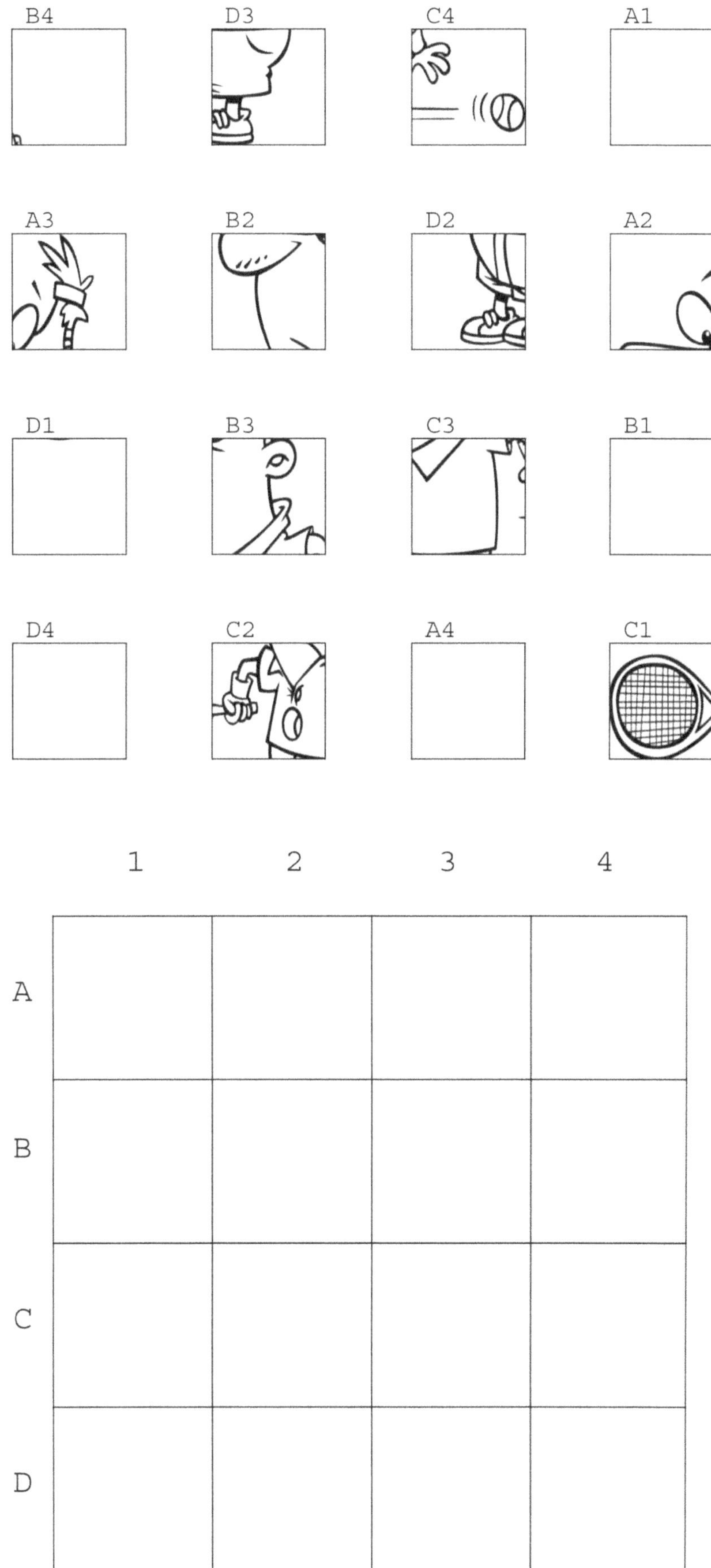

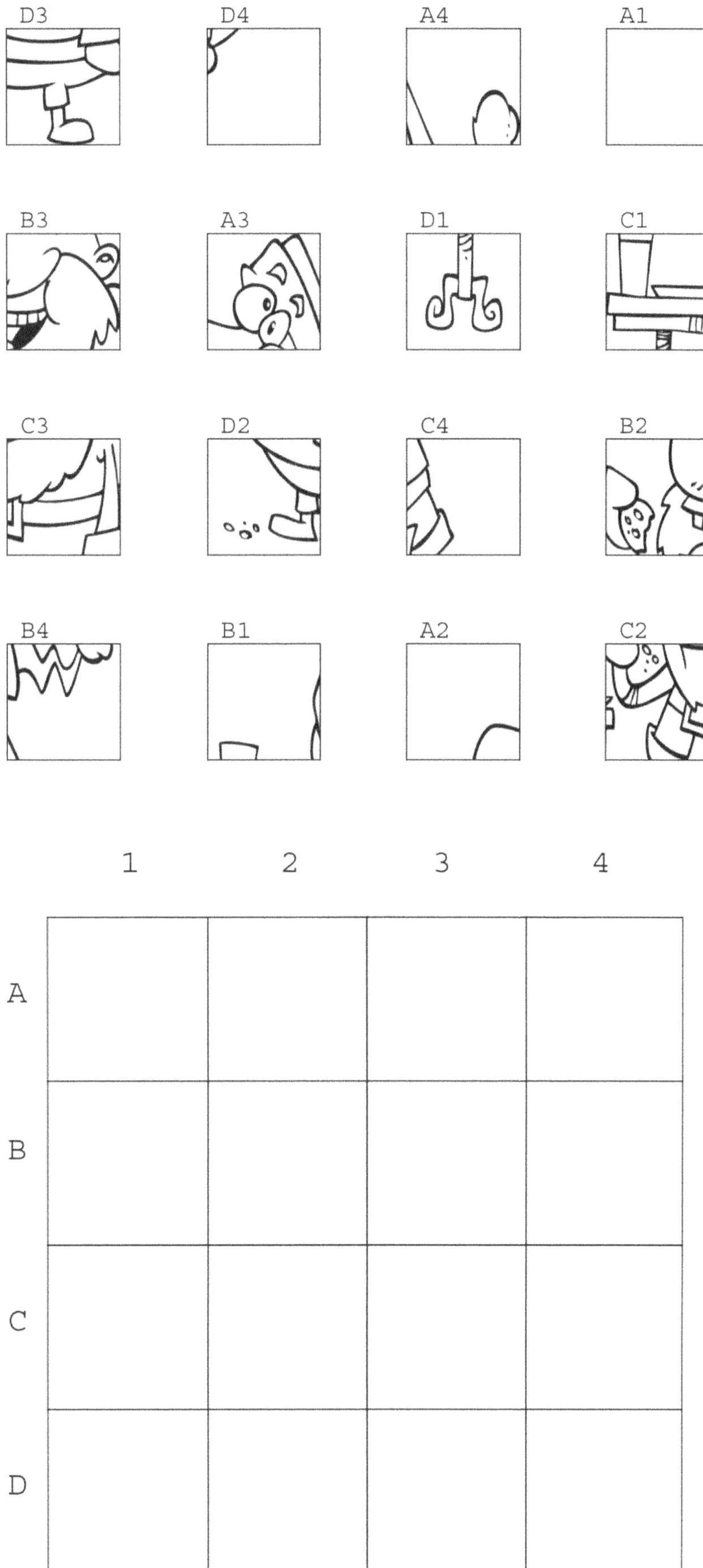

Thank you for completing our book! We appreciate your time and hope you enjoyed the experience. If you're up for more creative challenges, check out our other Pik-Jig books. Explore new grids and dive into the joy of artistic discovery. Happy drawing!

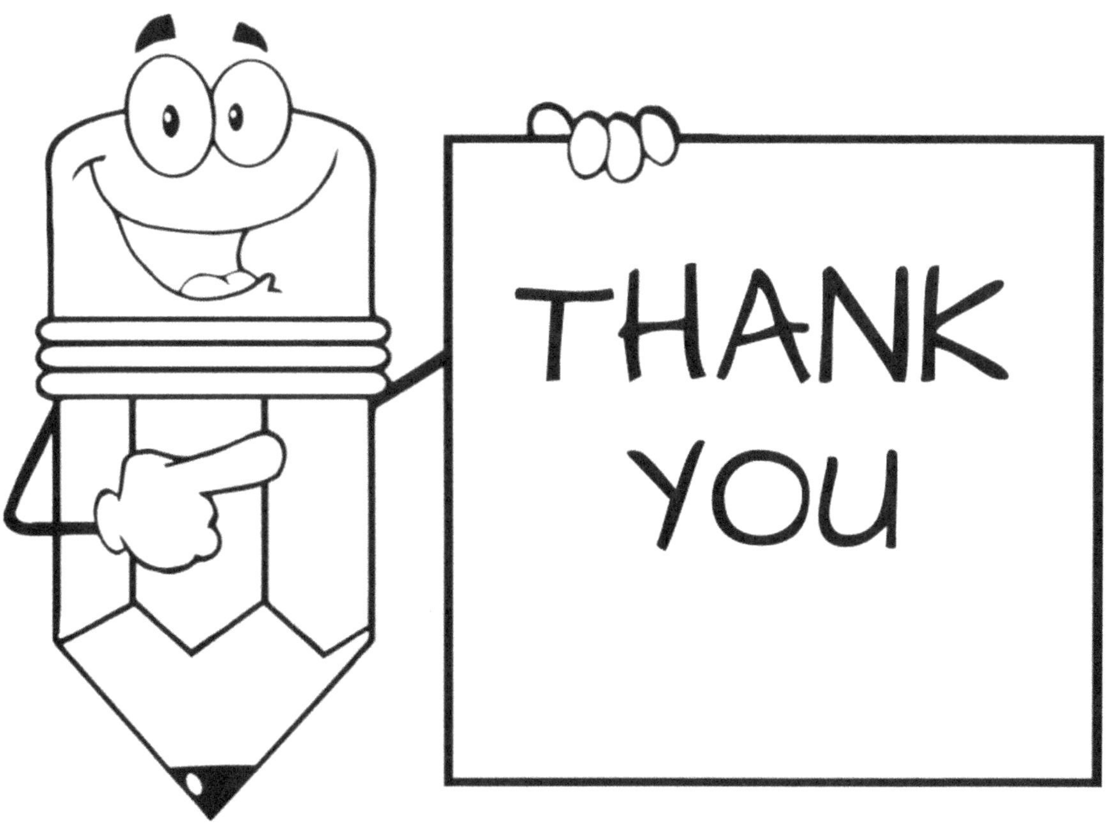